Hedonic Wage Equilibrium: Theory, Evidence and Policy

Hedonic Wage Equilibrium: Theory, Evidence and Policy

Thomas J. Kniesner

Syracuse University
USA
tkniesne@maxwell.syr.edu

IZA
Germany

John D. Leeth

Bentley University
USA
jleeth@bentley.edu

now
the essence of knowledge
Boston – Delft

Foundations and Trends® in Microeconomics

Published, sold and distributed by:
now Publishers Inc.
PO Box 1024
Hanover, MA 02339
USA
Tel. +1-781-985-4510
www.nowpublishers.com
sales@nowpublishers.com

Outside North America:
now Publishers Inc.
PO Box 179
2600 AD Delft
The Netherlands
Tel. +31-6-51115274

The preferred citation for this publication is T. J. Kniesner and J. D. Leeth, Hedonic Wage Equilibrium: Theory, Evidence and Policy, Foundations and Trends® in Microeconomics, vol 5, no 4, pp 229–299, 2009

ISBN: 978-1-60198-370-1

Foundations and Trends® in Microeconomics
Volume 5 Issue 4, 2009

Editorial Board

Editorial Scope

Foundations and Trends® in Microeconomics will publish survey and tutorial articles in the following topics:

- Environmental Economics
- Contingent Valuation
- Environmental Health Risks
- Climate Change
- Endangered Species
- Market-based Policy Instruments
- Health Economics
- Moral Hazard
- Medical Care Markets
- Medical Malpractice
- Insurance economics
- Industrial Organization
- Theory of the Firm
- Regulatory Economics
- Market Structure
- Auctions
- Monopolies and Antitrust
- Transaction Cost Economics
- Labor Economics
- Labor Supply
- Labor Demand
- Labor Market Institutions
- Search Theory
- Wage Structure
- Income Distribution
- Race and Gender
- Law and Economics
- Models of Litigation
- Crime
- Torts, Contracts and Property
- Constitutional Law
- Public Economics
- Public Goods
- Environmental Taxation
- Social Insurance
- Public Finance
- International Taxation

Information for Librarians

Foundations and Trends® in Microeconomics, 2009, Volume 5, 8 issues. ISSN paper version 1547-9846. ISSN online version 1547-9854. Also available as a combined paper and online subscription.

Foundations and Trends® in
Microeconomics
Vol. 5, No. 4 (2009) 229–299

DOI: 10.1561/0700000005

now
the essence of knowledge

Hedonic Wage Equilibrium: Theory, Evidence and Policy

Thomas J. Kniesner[1,2] and John D. Leeth[3]

[1] *Syracuse University, USA tkniesne@maxwell.syr.edu*
[2] *IZA, Germany*
[3] *Bentley University, USA jleeth@bentley.edu*

Abstract

We examine theoretically and empirically the properties of the equilibrium wage function and its implications for policy. Our emphasis is on how the researcher approaches economic and policy questions when there is labor market heterogeneity leading to a set of wages. We focus on the application where hedonic models have been most successful at clarifying policy relevant outcomes and policy effects that of the wage premia for fatal injury risk.

Estimates of the overall hedonic locus we discuss imply the so-called value of a statistical life (VSL) that is useful as the benefit value in a cost-effectiveness calculation of government programs to enhance personal safety. Additional econometric results described are the multiple dimensions of heterogeneity in VSL, including by age and consumption plans, the latent trait that affects wages and job safety setting choice, and family income.

Simulations of hedonic market outcomes are also valuable research tools. To demonstrate the additional usefulness of giving detail to the underlying structure we not only develop the issue of welfare comparisons theoretically, but also illustrate how numerical simulations of the underlying structure can also be informative. Using a reasonable set of primitives we see that job safety regulations are much more limited in their potential for improving workplace safety efficiently compared to mandatory injury insurance with experience rated premiums. The simulations reveal how regulations incent some workers to take more dangerous jobs, while workers' compensation insurance does not (or less so).

Contents

1

Labor-Market Equilibrium with Differented Workplaces

In the standard labor market model all workers are identical, all firms are identical, and a single wage equalizes the quantities of labor supplied and demanded. If the wage is too low then the excess demand for workers drives the wage up, while if the wage is too high the excess supply of workers drives the wage down. When workplaces differ in terms of non-wage job attributes the process describing labor market equilibrium is more complicated. Instead of a single wage, a wage function equilibrates the quantity of labor supplied to the quantity demanded at or near possible values of the attribute (Rosen, 1974). Here we examine theoretically and empirically the properties of the equilibrium wage function. Our focus is on the set of research and policy questions one can examine with enriched representation of labor market equilibrium, that is a set of wages caused by firm and worker heterogeneity.

Economists label the equilibrium relationship between wages and job attributes a hedonic equilibrium wage function. The logic behind the label is that wages reflect not only the overall conditions in the labor market but also the relative attractiveness (pleasure) of one job versus another. The underlying force generating the hedonic wage function is the sorting of workers and firms among the various levels of the job characteristic. To simplify our discussion suppose that all employers offer identical hours of work, and workers accept employment in only one firm. Further, we focus on a single job characteristic, z, which can be measured continuously and is a job disamenity, such as danger, heat, noise, stress, or poor fringe benefits.

In the remainder of Section 1 we lay out the complete economic structure of the hedonic labor market equilibrium model emphasizing the additional complexity and economic richness created by firms who differ in the production technologies and workers who differ in their attitudes toward risk. The remainder of Section 1 considers the possibility of multiple hedonic equilibrium loci for highly distinctive groups of workers such as smokers and nonsmokers and the hedonic locus for desirable workplace attributes.

Having established the basics of labor market outcomes under heterogeneity in Section 1, we proceed in Section 2 to describe the precision one can bring to policy evaluations with the hedonic equilibrium locus versus that with knowledge of the underlying fundamentals, such as an individual's indifference curve revealing the worker' willingness to pay for a better working environment. The reader interested mainly in learning the fundamentals of hedonic equilibrium can focus on Sections 1 and 2 only.

As a complement to Section 2, Section 3 describes the special econometric issues involved with estimating the hedonic locus and the underlying structure resulting from worker and firm heterogeneity and the implicit prices of workplace characteristics that are the fundamental ingredients to a hedonic equilibrium econometric model. The reader who is knowledgeable in the theoretical dimension of hedonic equilibrium, but who wants to learn the econometric nuances of the model, can focus on Section 3.

Section 4 presents recent empirical results for the hedonic wage equilibrium locus and their implications for policy that use the value of a statistical life (VSL), which is the implicit value workers as a group place on one life. Section 4 is a standalone presentation that may be the primary interest of readers knowledgeable in how to estimate hedonic equilibrium regression models but want to learn some useful recent econometric results. In particular, Section 4 begins with questions of whether there is a simple way to get distributional issues into the model via a person's relative position in the wage distribution and whether relative position is an empirically more important issue than the worker's age. The effect of aging on the worker's implicit pay for accepting a fatal injury risk will depend on consumption plans and we provide estimates of the importance of planned consumption in equilibrium wage outcomes. Both relative position and consumption are forms of worker measured heterogeneity and we supplement the heterogeneity issue in Section 4 with results for latent worker heterogeneity. Our econometric evidence is that accounting for latent worker heterogeneity that may be correlated with job safety risk is the single most important dimension of an econometric model of hedonic wage equilibrium. Accounting for latent heterogeneity greatly narrows the range of VSL estimates and clarifies the cost-effectiveness of life-saving policies. The issue presented in Section 4 is a formal regression model of differences in the effect of fatal injury on the wage by expected wage level. Using quantile regression with latent individual heterogeneity included discovers wealth effects in the value of a statistical life that are policy relevant and also makes the econometric results now consistent with economic theory, which has not formerly been the case.

Econometric estimates are not the only way to give empirical content to the hedonic model. In Section 5 we present the empirical alternative of numerical simulation, which may be the focal section for readers well versed in the theory and econometrics but wish to expand their knowledge base to include the technique of computable hedonic equilibrium. Specifically, in Section 5 we numerically simulate the complete hedonic model developed in Section 1. By parameterizing the underlying structure of the model we are able to examine large and complex changes in workplace safety policy that would be poorly estimated by an econometric model due to extrapolation bias and latent parameters. Our results show the relative dominance of workers' compensation insurance over occupational safety and health regulations in improving workplace safety.

Section 6 concludes.

1.1 Firms

Programs to improve workplace conditions or fringe benefits (lower z) are costly. An employer must anticipate corresponding economic benefits, such as greater output, lower pay for workers, smaller insurance premiums, or lower fines for violating government standards to be willing to bear their additional costs.[1] The economic problem confronting the employer is to choose the combination of capital, labor, and workplace environment that maximizes profit subject to $z \geq 0$. To reduce the complexity of the discussion we assume a standard device exists that monotonically decreases the workplace disamenity. We refer to the generic device, which represents all the firm's efforts to improve the work environment, as work environment equipment. Revenue is a function of capital, labor, and work environment equipment. Input cost includes the wage bill plus the cost of capital. Also included are the cost of work environment equipment, the cost of workers' insurance (health, workers compensation, and disability), and possible fines for violating government workplace standards, which are avenues for government policy that we will ultimately explore.

Algebraically, profit is:

$$\Pi = R(n,k,E(z);\mu) - W(z)n - p_k k - p_e E(z) - P_i(z)n - V(z), \tag{1.1}$$

where $\Pi \equiv$ profit,
$R(\cdot) \equiv$ the revenue function,
$n \equiv$ the number of workers,
$k \equiv$ the quantity of capital,
$e \equiv$ the quantity of work environment equipment,
$e = E(z)$; $E(\cdot)$ is the work environment function and $\partial E/\partial z \equiv E' < 0$,

[1] Programs geared to reducing workplace disamenities may increase or decrease production. Reducing disamenities such as heat and noise could improve worker productivity and expand output. In the case of workplace injuries, Viscusi (1979) argues that greater safety raises output by diminishing the disruptive effects of accidents and by increasing the stability of the workforce. Alternatively, slowing the pace of the assembly line or installing cumbersome machine guards can interfere with the work process and decrease output. For purposes of the theoretical derivation of hedonic equilibrium we assume that reductions in workplace disamenities raise output.

$\mu \equiv$ a parameter representing the efficiency of work environment equipment in the production of output $(\partial^2 R/\partial e \partial \mu > 0)$,

$W(z) \equiv$ the market wage function, $\partial W/\partial z \equiv W' > 0$,

$p_k \equiv$ the per-unit price of capital,

$p_e \equiv$ the per-unit price of work environment equipment,

$p_i \equiv$ the per-worker price of health, disability, and workers compensation insurance, $p_i = P_i(z)$; $P_i(\cdot)$ is the insurance pricing function with $\partial P_i/\partial z \equiv P' > 0$, and

$V(z) \equiv$ the expected fine for violating workplace standards, $\partial V/\partial z \equiv V' > 0$.

Labor, capital, and work environment equipment each increase revenue at decreasing rates, and all cross derivatives among labor, capital, and work environment equipment are positive. Note that $W(z)$ need not be an equilibrium wage function as yet; workers and firms need only observe and make their decisions based on the relationship between wages and the job disamenity.

Managers influence profit through their decisions on hiring labor, purchasing capital, and purchasing work environment-improving equipment (reducing workplace disamenities). All three decisions must be made jointly to maximize profit; decreasing disamenities increases the productivity of labor and capital, while increasing labor and capital increases the net benefits from improving the work environment. By differentiating Equation (1.1) with respect to n, k, and z, setting each result equal to zero and rearranging terms, we can show the firm's optimal usage of each input occurs when:

$$\frac{\partial R}{\partial n} = W(z) + P_i(z), \tag{1.2}$$

$$\frac{\partial R}{\partial k} = p_k, \quad \text{and} \tag{1.3}$$

$$\frac{\partial R}{\partial E} E' - W'n - P'n - V' = p_e E'. \tag{1.4}$$

Firms increase their use of labor and capital until the expected marginal revenue product of each input equals its expected marginal cost. In addition, firms reduce workplace disamenities until the marginal benefit — greater output, lower wages, lower insurance costs, and smaller government fines — equals the marginal cost of purchasing more work environment equipment. Because the output effect of work environment equipment varies among workplaces the marginal benefits of reducing workplace disamenities differ among firms, in turn causing the optimum level of the disamenity to vary. Firms where work environment-improving measures are highly productive reduce disamenities more than firms where improving the work environment is less productive.

The situation facing the firm can be viewed graphically. A firm's offer wage function (isoprofit curve) shows the tradeoff between wages and workplace disamenities at a constant level of expected profit with capital and labor used in optimal quantities. To keep the same level of profit, wages must fall as work disamenities decrease to compensate for the added cost of purchasing work environment equipment so that offer wage functions slope upward. Firms with greater costs of producing a pleasant workplace require a greater wage reduction to lower disamenities than firms with smaller costs of producing a pleasant work environment, all else equal. The firm with the higher marginal cost of producing a better workplace will have a more steeply sloped offer wage function at a given wage and work disamenity than a firm with a lower marginal cost. Finally, profits rise as wages fall implying the lower the offer wage function the higher the profit.

Figure 1.1 shows the market wage function and offer wage functions for two companies. As can be seen, Company A maximizes profit by offering workers job attributes equal to z^A, the level where the offer wage function is just tangent to the hedonic wage function. Because its costs of providing an amenity such as a pleasant or safe work environment are greater, Company B maximizes profit by offering a less agreeable job, z^{B}, but paying higher wages than Company A to compensate workers for the less pleasant working conditions. With a sufficiently large number of diverse firms each point on the hedonic wage function represents a point of tangency for some company or companies. The hedonic wage function represents an upper envelope of a family of offer wage curves that differ because of the variation in the technical ability of firms to produce pleasant work environments. It slopes

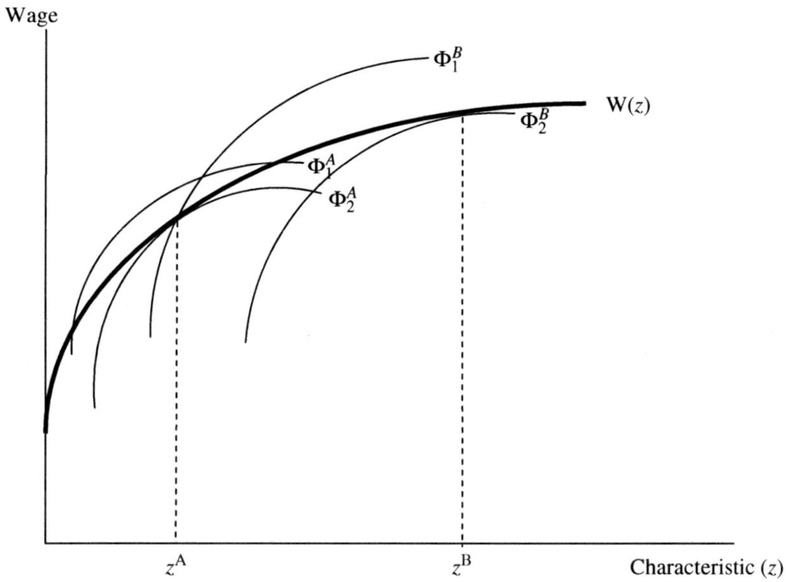

Fig. 1.1 Firm equilibrium.

upward because firms are willing to pay higher wages to avoid bearing the added expenses of providing better working conditions.

1.2 Workers

The problem confronting a worker is to find the level of consumption and workplace disamenity that maximizes utility subject to the overall budget constraint. In the situation we are considering the mathematical representation of utility is:

$$u = U(c, z; \alpha), \tag{1.5}$$

where $u \equiv$ the utility index,
$U(\cdot) \equiv$ the worker's utility function with $\partial U/\partial c > 0$ and $\partial U/\partial z < 0$,
$c \equiv$ consumption,
$z \equiv$ the workplace attribute, and
$\alpha \equiv$ a parameter determining workers' preferences regarding z.

In this representation $U(\cdot)$ represents a standard utility function with the workplace attribute, z, differing from normal consumption items, c, only in the sense that z is directly provided by employers and c is purchased by workers in an open market. Many hedonic wage studies and much of our later analysis examine workplace risk as the job characteristic. When examining a stochastic job attribute such as the likelihood of a workplace injury or fatality it is natural to use a Von Neumann–Morgenstern expected utility function to represent preferences. The analysis we develop is quite general and can easily be modified to examine stochastic workplace attributes using a Von Neumann–Morgenstern approach (see, for instance, Kniesner and Leeth, 1995b; Viscusi and Hersch, 2001; Viscusi and Aldy, 2003).

Remember $W(\pi)$ in Equation (1.5) represents the market wage function, observable to workers and firms, and y is non-labor income, so that consumption is $c = W(z) + y$. By substituting the expression for c into Equation (1.5), differentiating with respect to z, setting the result equal to 0, and then rearranging we can show that a worker's optimal level of z is when:

$$\frac{\partial U}{\partial c} W' = -\frac{\partial U}{\partial z}. \tag{1.6}$$

The story here is the standard one where a worker weighs the marginal benefit of a higher level of a workplace disamenity against the marginal cost. The left-hand side of Equation (1.6) represents the marginal benefit, which is the added pay from a more disagreeable job, and the right-hand side of Equation (1.6) represents the marginal cost, which is the direct loss of utility from the job disamenity. Because preferences differ among workers the perceived marginal gain and cost differ among them too, in turn causing the optimal level of z to vary. Interpersonal differences or heterogeneity is a fundamental dimension of labor market hedonics. Workers with a strong distaste for z sort into jobs with low workplace disamenities, and workers with only a mild distaste for z sort into jobs with high workplace disamenities.

Similar to the situation for firms, workers' decisions regarding the disamenity can also be clarified graphically. A worker's acceptance wage function (indifference curve) illustrates the tradeoff between wages and

z at a constant level of utility. To maintain a specific level of well-being wages must rise to compensate for bearing a higher amount of a bad job characteristic, so acceptance wage functions slope upward. Additionally, workers more averse to the disamenity require greater wage compensation for a given increase in z than workers less averse to the disamenity, all else equal, so the worker with the steeper acceptance wage function at a given (W, z) is the more averse to the job attribute. Lastly, workers prefer higher wages to lower wages at any level of the attribute, so the higher the acceptance wage function the higher the utility. The choice of the optimal level of z can be viewed similarly to the choice of the optimal purchase of commodities with the market wage function replacing the standard income constraint.

Figure 1.2 portrays acceptance wage functions for two workers in relation to a market wage function. We see Worker C maximizing utility by selecting a job offering attributes equal to z^{C}. The highest level of utility the worker can achieve occurs where the acceptance wage function is just tangent to the market wage curve. Although z^{C} maximizes

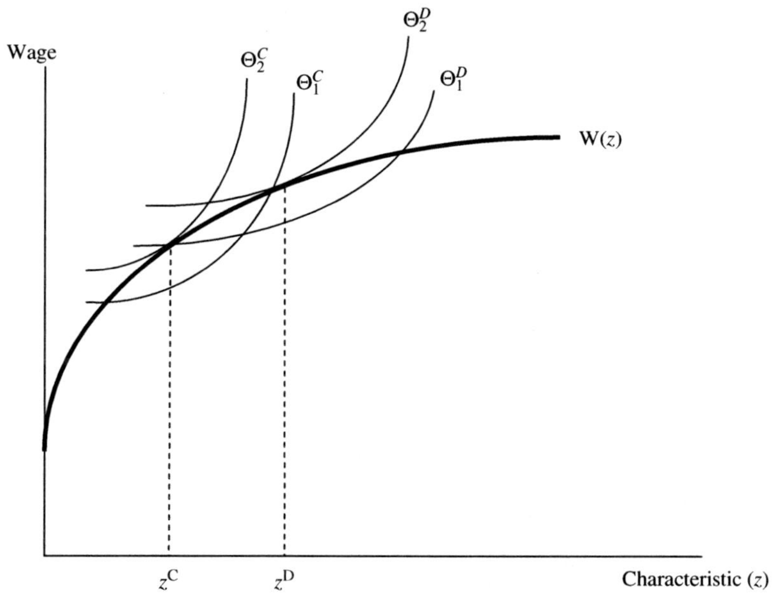

Fig. 1.2 Worker equilibrium.

Worker C's utility, it does not maximize Worker D's utility; Worker D requires a smaller increase in wages to accept a slight rise in workplace disamenities, utility held constant. Worker D maximizes utility by choosing a slightly more disagreeable job, characterized by z^{D}, and earning a higher wage. With a sufficiently large number of diverse workers, each point on the hedonic wage function is a point of tangency for some group of workers. In technical language, the wage function represents the lower envelope of a family of acceptance wage curves, which differ because workers vary in their attitudes regarding z.

1.3 Labor Market Equilibrium

Firms supply a given type of workplace based on the market wage function and their ability to produce the attribute. Workers sort into a given job type (z) based on the market (hedonic) wage function and their preferences regarding the job attribute. The hedonic wage function equilibrates the supply and demand for labor along the entire job attribute spectrum. A shortage of workers in high-z establishments, for instance, will drive up wages, thereby enticing some workers away from more pleasant employment. At the same time, the wage hike will encourage some firms to expand their expenditures on workplace improvements to reduce labor costs. With workers moving toward greater z, and firms moving toward less z, wages must rise in relatively more desirable workplaces. An excess demand for labor at any point along the job attribute spectrum alters the delicate balancing of labor supply and demand everywhere. Wages adjust until the supply of labor equals the demand for labor along the entire spectrum.

The slope of the acceptance wage function measures the wage a worker is willing to sacrifice to reduce job disamenities by a small amount and, therefore, provides a dollar figure of worker's willingness to pay for job attributes implicitly. At the same time, the slope of the isoprofit curve measures the reduction in wages required by a firm to compensate for the higher costs of improving the work environment. As can be seen in Figure 1.3, the hedonic wage function maps out a set of tangencies between workers' acceptance wage functions and firms' isoprofit curves or offer wage functions.

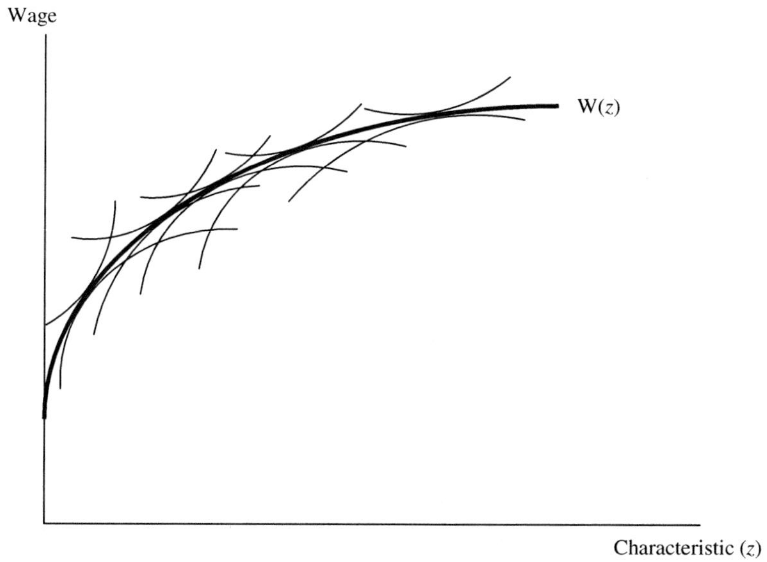

Fig. 1.3 Hedonic labor market equilibrium.

Although firms could reduce z below the various levels shown in Figure 1.3, thereby improving the work environment, the benefits would be less than the costs. The small wage reduction would not compensate for the added expenses. Workers could likewise improve their work environment by accepting employment at a firm offering a lower z. They choose not to because the wage sacrifice exceeds the value they place on a more pleasant environment. This is not to say workers dislike a nice work setting. They simply like *both* a pleasant workplace and income, so they willingly make tradeoffs between amenities and income. In equilibrium, the monetary sacrifice workers are willing to make for additional amenities just equals firms' costs of providing additional amenities.

The hedonic wage function balances the supply and demand for labor along the entire job attribute spectrum. The equilibrium wage function here must satisfy the following condition (Rosen, 1974):

$$L(\alpha)\left|\frac{d\alpha}{dz}\right| dz = N(\mu)F(\mu)\left|\frac{d\mu}{dz}\right| dz, \tag{1.7}$$

where $L(\cdot) \equiv$ the density function of workers with respect to α, with $\alpha_{\min} \leq \alpha \leq \alpha_{\max}$,

$N(\cdot) \equiv$ the demand for labor by an individual firm, and
$F(\cdot) \equiv$ the density function of firms with respect to μ, with $\mu_{\min} \leq \mu \leq \mu_{\max}$.

The differentials $d\alpha/dz$ and $d\mu/dz$ depict the sorting of workers and firms into levels of z, which is the mapping of acceptance and offer wage functions along the market wage function in Figure 1.3. The left-hand side of Equation (1.7) represents the number of workers supplying labor to firms with a given level of safety while the right-hand side of Equation (1.7) represents the demand for workers. Because labor supplied and demanded must be identical in equilibrium we can use Equation (1.7) to describe the equilibrium sorting of workers by job attribute. By totally differentiating the first-order conditions for the maximization of profit with respect to μ (treating it as an endogenous variable) we can develop an expression for the equilibrium sorting of firm characteristics by job attribute (see Equations (1.2)–(1.4)). We can then determine the increase in wages necessary for workers to accept a given job attribute (dw/dz) using the first-order conditions for utility maximization (see Equation (1.6)). A system of three simultaneous first-order differential equations completely describing hedonic equilibrium in the labor market is:

$$\frac{d\alpha}{dz} = A'(z,\alpha,\mu,w,M'), \tag{1.8}$$

$$\frac{d\mu}{dz} = M'(z,\alpha,\mu,w,A',W'), \quad \text{and} \tag{1.9}$$

$$\frac{dw}{dz} = W'(z,\alpha,w). \tag{1.10}$$

In hedonic equilibrium the first-order conditions for utility and profit maximization are satisfied, and the labor market is in equilibrium at all levels of job attributes. The three differential Equations (1.8), (1.9), and (1.10) determine the relationship between worker characteristics and z, between firm characteristics and z, and the hedonic wage function. Boundary conditions determine the minimum μ and the maximum z observed in the labor market as well as establish equilibrium at the two endpoints of the attribute spectrum.

1.4 Segmented Labor Markets

Not everyone in the labor market may face the same hedonic wage function. The hedonic wage function can differ across groups because of discrimination or because of observable differences in productivity. In a notable study, Viscusi and Hersch (2001) examine the wage–workplace risk functions facing smokers and nonsmokers. Smoking is dangerous, so one would expect the greater risk tolerance of smokers (flatter acceptance wage functions) would cause them to locate further to the right along the hedonic wage locus. In Figure 1.4 smokers would locate at job risk π_2 and nonsmokers at job risk π_1. If smokers and nonsmokers face the same hedonic wage function then smokers who bear more workplace risk earn a higher premium for risk than nonsmokers.

If smokers earn a smaller risk premium for bearing more risk than nonsmokers then they must face a lower, flatter hedonic wage function than nonsmokers such as the one labeled smokers in Figure 1.4. Examining the size of risk premiums for different groups provides a strong test of a segmented labor market. As shown in Figure 1.4 the risk premium for nonsmokers, $w^n(\pi_1) - w^n(0)$, where $w^n(0)$ is the wage rate with zero job risk, exceeds the risk premium of smokers, $w^s(\pi_2) - w^s(0)$. Such a segmented labor market can occur if employers are able to identify groups of workers who are less efficient at producing the job characteristic in question. Besides more workplace injuries, smokers have more accidents at home than nonsmokers, implying a lower ability to produce safety, which makes it desirable for employers to offer them a smaller wage gain for accepting more risk. Viscusi and Hersch find that smokers earn a smaller risk premium than nonsmokers although their risk of injury is higher, demonstrating that they face a hedonic wage function that is lower and flatter than the one facing nonsmokers, such as in Figure 1.4.

Other studies also find evidence of segmented labor markets. Blacks face a lower, flatter hedonic wage function for workplace fatalities than whites (Viscusi, 2003) and Mexican immigrants to the United States face a lower, flatter hedonic wage function for workplace fatalities than U.S. natives (Viscusi and Hersch, 2010).

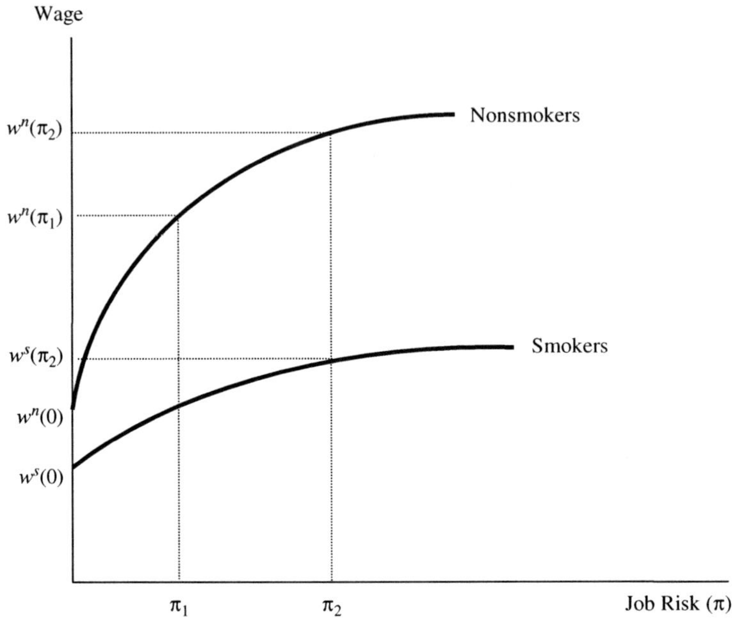

Fig. 1.4 Hedonic wage functions for smokers and nonsmokers.

1.5 Desirable Job Attributes

Our discussion to now has described the situation where workers face a disagreeable job characteristic such as poor fringe benefits; an increased danger of an injury or illness; an extremely noisy, hot, dusty, or otherwise unpleasant workplace; more frequent spells of unemployment; or overly rigid work hours. If worker utility falls with higher levels of the attribute in question and costs rise when firms attempt to eliminate the attribute, then the hedonic wage function will be upward sloping as in Figure 1.3. On the other hand, if workers get utility from the attribute ($\partial U/\partial z > 0$), and costs rise as firms provide the attribute, as would be the case with fringe benefits, then the hedonic wage function would slope downward. Defining z as a positive job attribute does not alter the underlying thought process of hedonic equilibrium, although it does alter the final conclusion concerning the sign of the relationship between wages and the attribute. However, any negative job attribute can be redefined as a positive attribute and vice versa;

instead of workplace safety, workplace danger; instead of pleasant working conditions, unpleasant working conditions; and instead of flexible work hours, inflexible work hours. In some cases it is more natural to think of the job attribute as a negative condition of employment and in other cases as a positive condition of employment. When the attribute is framed as a positive condition, a job amenity, wages fall as the amount of the attribute rises. Workers sacrifice wage income for the desirable job characteristic, and the lower wage costs compensate firms for the higher costs of providing the job characteristic.

2

Evaluating Policy Changes

Evaluating policy changes aimed at improving the workplace require estimates of costs and benefits. Cost estimates are usually generated through accounting or engineering studies. Although disagreements may arise over assumptions made by analysts the overall approach is non-controversial. Determining the benefits of reducing a workplace or environmental disamenity requires placing a monetary value on the disamenity. Although several approaches exist economists most frequently rely on estimates of the hedonic wage function to determine benefits. They use their estimates to answer the question, how much will people be willing to pay to reduce their exposure to the disamenity in question by a small amount?

Figure 2.1 shows that the actual monetary value Worker A places on reducing the disamenity from z^1 to z^2 can be found by tracing out the wage change along the worker's indifference curve as the disamenity falls. Based on the numbers in the graph, Worker A would be indifferent between a salary of \$12,000 and z^1 of the disamenity or a salary of \$11,800 and z^2 of the disamenity. The worker values the improvement in the workplace by \$200. Economists are rarely able to estimate the indifference curves underlying hedonic equilibrium, so they cannot

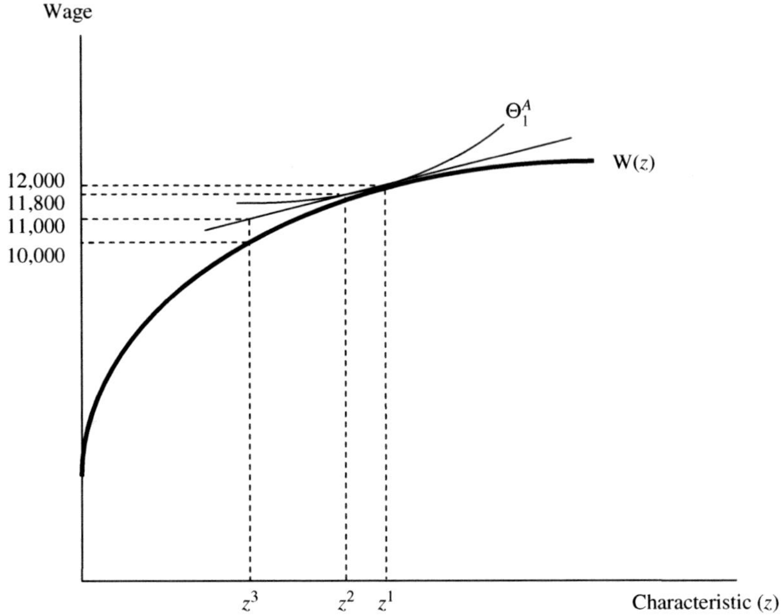

Fig. 2.1 Placing a monetary value on a workplace disamenity.

directly calculate benefit changes.[1] Instead they approximate the wage change along the indifference curve by using the hedonic wage function itself.

In equilibrium, the slope of the hedonic wage function equals the slope of the indifference curves of workers choosing the various levels of the disamenity. For small changes in z, $W'\ dz$ reasonably approximates the reduction in wage along the indifference curve. The \$200 wage reduction moving down the tangent line in Figure 2.1 from z^1 to z^2 is only slightly larger than the wage reduction along the indifference curve. For large reductions in z the approximation substantially overstates the value workers place on the disamenity, as can be seen in the graph. The first derivative approach suggests workers like A place a

[1] For a notable attempt see Viscusi and Evans (1990), who use survey data on reservation wages for a higher risk level coupled with information on the worker's current wage and risk to infer the marginal value of injury prevention. More recently, Sojourner (2010) applies recently developed statistical bounding techniques to examine the properties of a worker's indifference curve where there is a tradeoff between pay and fatal injury risk at work.

\$1,000 value on reducing the disamenity from z^1 to z^3, when in actuality the movement along the indifference curve suggests that they value the improvement by only slightly more than \$200. In the other direction, the slope of the tangent line underestimates the costs of a serious deterioration in the work environment. The rise in wage necessary to maintain worker welfare moving to the right along the indifference curve is considerably larger than the movement along the tangent line.

In a policy context the slope of the hedonic wage function overestimates the benefits of workplace improvements, but for firms evaluating the profitability of improving their own workplaces the slope of the hedonic wage function may underestimate the benefits. The firm's existing workers would be willing to accept a wage cut of only slightly more than \$200 for a drop in the disamenity from z^1 to z^3 as shown by the movement along the indifference curve. A firm who knew worker preferences and was interested in retaining its current employees would compare the costs of reducing z to the benefits of reducing wages by slightly more than \$200 per worker and make the necessary improvements if benefits exceeded costs. Alternatively, a firm may not know worker preferences and rely on the slope of the hedonic wage function to value the wage cuts it can make by improving workplace conditions. In this case, the \$1,000 movement along the tangent line overestimates the wage cut the firm can make if it wishes to retain its current workers but underestimates the wage cut the firm can initiate if it is willing to hire new workers. Workers who value workplace amenities more highly than the current employees will accept a wage/disamenity combination of \$10,000/z^1 as shown by the hedonic function, meaning the benefit of improving workplace conditions is \$2,000 per worker, not \$1,000, if the firm is willing to hire new workers. The slope of the tangent line underestimates the value to the firm of improving workplace conditions.

An additional issue in evaluating policies geared at reducing workplace disamenities (or increasing amenities) is the impact of the policy on hedonic equilibrium. If the policy affects only a few workers or a few firms the change is unlikely to alter market conditions markedly, leaving the hedonic equilibrium locus constant. If the policy affects many workers and firms, however, the relocation of workers and firms alters the balancing of supply and demand resulting in a new locus, which may reinforce or mitigate the initial welfare effects.

The impact on the hedonic equilibrium locus is frequently ignored in policy evaluations. In their discussions of the Occupational Safety and Health Administration (OSHA) Borjas (2010) and Ehrenberg and Smith (2009), for example, show fully informed workers harmed by health and safety standards that eliminate extremely risky jobs without considering any feedback effects of the regulations on hedonic equilibrium. In Figure 2.2, the hedonic wage function maps out the relationship between wages and the probability of an accident or disease on the job. In the absence of OSHA, the highest indifference curve Worker A can reach is the one just tangent to the hedonic function at the probability of injury (π^1) and wage (w^1). On the other side of the market the lowest isoprofit curve (the highest level of profit) Firm C can reach is the one just tangent to the wage curve at the probability of injury (π^1) and wage (w^1). Assume OSHA regulations require all firms

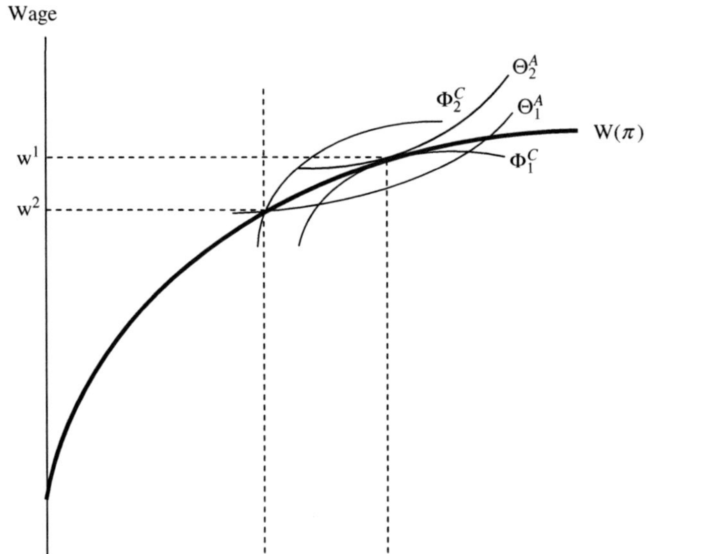

Fig. 2.2 The welfare impact of OSHA with no changes in hedonic equilibrium.

install enough safety equipment so the chance of injury is no greater than $\pi^{\max}$. All firms originally offering higher risk jobs, such as Firm C, will install additional safety equipment reducing the chance of injury to $\pi^{\max}$. Although the improvement in safety allows the firm to lower wages to w^2, the lower labor expenses fail to outweigh the higher costs of safety equipment and profits fall from $\mathbf{\Phi_1}$ to $\mathbf{\Phi_2}$. With the high-risk jobs eliminated workers, like A, accept employment at the safer worksites but earn lower wages. The reduction in wage more than offsets the improvement in safety and utility falls from $\mathbf{\Theta_1}$ to $\mathbf{\Theta_2}$. OSHA reduces both firm profits and worker welfare initially.

Based on the above analysis, OSHA or any policy mandating minimum workplace standards lowers profits for firms originally offering a less agreeable workplace, lowers the welfare of workers who choose work in the less agreeable workplaces, and leaves everyone else equally well off. The difficulty with the analysis so far is that it ignores the impact of the policy on the hedonic wage function. Improving working conditions reduces profits causing some firms to shut down and fire their workers. In the other direction, the improvement in working conditions means other firms can pay a lower wage, which causes them to expand hiring. The improvements may also directly affect labor productivity. If productivity rises, then the firms moving to $\pi^{\max}$ will expand hiring even more. On the worker side the loss of welfare from working may cause some workers to exit the labor market. The drop in wage also creates income and substitution effects that alter the number of hours workers are willing to supply. With the demand for labor and the supply of labor changing it is very unlikely the wage will remain constant at $\pi^{\max}$, and any wage change at $\pi^{\max}$ will disequilibrate the entire balancing of supply and demand along the entire characteristic spectrum.

In numerical simulations Kniesner and Leeth (1988, 1989a) examine the impact of OSHA in a more complete equilibrium context. In their simulations OSHA regulations raise and flatten the hedonic wage function. Regulations and associated penalties for non-compliance encourages firms to expand safety efforts and move to the left along the hedonic wage function. To restore equilibrium workers must also move to the left. Safety is a normal good so the increase in income from the hedonic function rising causes workers to desire safer employment.

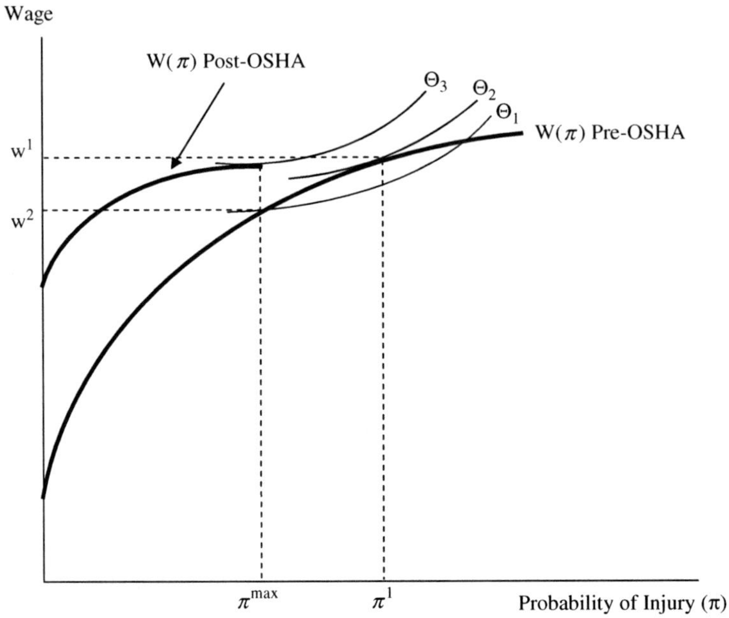

Fig. 2.3 The welfare impact of OSHA with changes in hedonic equilibrium.

The flattening of the hedonic function also means the added compensation for accepting job hazards is lower causing workers to desire safer jobs.

As can be seen in Figure 2.3, prior to OSHA Worker A accepts employment with a high chance of injury (π^1). OSHA regulations increase firms' costs of accidents and diseases and reduce the maximum observed chance of injury on the job to $\pi^{\max}$. If the hedonic wage function remained the same then Worker A's welfare would fall from $\boldsymbol{\Theta}_\mathbf{2}$ to $\boldsymbol{\Theta}_\mathbf{1}$, but the function rises and becomes flatter allowing the worker to reach a higher indifference curve, $\boldsymbol{\Theta}_\mathbf{3}$. Additionally, workers originally employed in relatively safe employment also receive wage increases as the wage function rises so their welfare improves. The higher labor costs reduce firm profitability, not only for high-risk workplaces but also for low-risk workplaces. Firms in turn cut back on production resulting in higher output prices and a loss of consumer surplus. Workers ultimately gain, and firms and consumers lose.

The point of the OSHA example just completed is to underscore that policy evaluations involving relative well-being outcomes require the underlying structural utility and production (cost) equations. How the researchers gets to them begins with the quantitative properties of the market hedonic wage locus.

3

Giving Empirical Content to Hedonic Outcomes

The bedrock of quantitative research on workplace attributes is econometric estimation. The canonical structural econometric model of the labor market where a sorting of workers into jobs yields a set of wage and job attribute levels for each job and worker. The stochastic model of hedonic labor market equilibrium outcome has three underlying stochastic equations

$$n_j^s = N^s(W'(z_j), x_j^s; \alpha_j) + \varepsilon_j^s, \tag{3.1}$$

$$n_j^d = N^d(W'(z_j), x_j^d; \mu_j) + \varepsilon_j^d, \quad \text{and} \tag{3.2}$$

$$w_j = W(z_j, x_j^L) + \varepsilon_j^L. \tag{3.3}$$

The last equation in the system (Equation (3.3)) is the hedonic equilibrium locus, summarizing how the wage rate indexed by j (which could indicate a person, industry, occupation, location, or year) varies with the job attribute (z) and characteristics that influence wage outcomes in the labor market (x^L). Equations (3.1) and (3.2) are the supply and demand for workers that produce the hedonic locus in Equation (3.3). The supply and demand for workers both depend on three things: (i) the marginal wage ($W'(z_j) \equiv \partial W(z_j)/\partial z$), which varies with z, (ii) the vectors of usual independent variables influencing the number of workers and jobs captured in x^s and x^d, such as households' wealth and firms' nonlabor input costs, and (iii) workers' attitudes toward the attribute as metered in the person-specific random variable α plus firms' efficiency in producing the attribute as summarized in the firm-specific random variable μ.

Estimating the supply schedule in Equation (3.1) identifies the parameters of workers' utility functions, and estimating the demand relation in Equation (3.2) identifies the parameters of the firms' production and cost functions. Each equation in Equations (3.1)–(3.3) plays a different role in determining the workplace attribute, and each equation has special statistical properties that make Equations (3.1)–(3.3) differ from the usual simultaneous equations system so that estimating the complete canonical hedonic labor market model is comparatively difficult.

3.1 Estimating the Hedonic Wage Locus

Economists use the hedonic locus summarized in Equation (3.3) to study employment patterns of how the labor market implicitly compensates workers for accepting job disamenities or implicitly charges workers for job amenities. In the case of workplace safety, the slope of the hedonic locus, $W'(z_j)$, is the marginal wage premium firms must pay workers to accept (more) injury risk and has been used to compute the implicit value workers place on their lives via risking death at work, which policy makers have used in program cost-effectiveness calculations. Other implicit values or costs of workplace characteristics that have been studied in the context of the hedonic equilibrium locus include fringe benefits, progressive income taxes, working conditions, and wage variability across people and over time. We now turn our attention to the econometric issues relating to estimating the hedonic wage locus followed by a tasting menu of empirical results.

3.2 Estimating Workers and Firms' Value Functions

For certain policy questions it is necessary to identify the objectives or so-called value functions that underlie the parameters of the supply and demand for workers in Equations (3.1) and (3.2). For example, if we want to draw inferences concerning how workers' well-being or firms' profits change due to more stringent OSHA regulations then we will need the parameters of utility functions and profit functions. There is an extensive theoretical econometric literature explaining why identifying the parameters of the structural equations in the canonical hedonic model in Equations (3.1)–(3.3) is more difficult than the standard simultaneous equations system, such as the supply and demand for a homogenous product such as milk (Brown and Rosen, 1982; Epple, 1987; Kahn and Lang, 1988). The primary reason that identifying the supply and demand equations underlying hedonic equilibrium models is so econometrically difficult is that the prices are implicit, rather than posted.

Although you can go to the grocery store or look in the newspaper to learn the price of eggs, the price of more desirable job characteristics is implicit in the wage structure. The hedonic wage Equation (3.3) not only describes the labor market in equilibrium but its parameter estimates are also what the econometrician must use to compute the implicit price of job attributes, $W'(z_j)$, which is then an independent variable in the supply and demand schedules (Equations (3.1) and (3.2)). A crucial consequence of having to manufacture econometrically the implicit price workers, pay for (the implicit costs to firms of providing) the job characteristic is that either $W(z_j, x_j^L)$ in Equation (3.3) must be highly nonlinear (for example, cubic in z) or some of the independent variables explaining the hedonic locus in x_j^L, such as region, cannot also explain either labor supply or demand (x_j^L must differ from x_j^s and x_j^d). The logic behind the restriction on the shape and explanatory variables of Equation (3.3) is that the hedonic wage function must contain information independent of supply and demand if the implied compensating wage differential $W'(z_j)$ computed from estimates of Equation (3.3) is to add additional information to the other arguments in supply and demand Equations (3.1) and (3.2) (Brown and Rosen, 1982).

Another econometric complexity in estimating a complete hedonic equilibrium model as summarized in Equations (3.1)–(3.3) happens because the level of the job attribute, z, is the result of optimizing decisions by firms and workers. The observed z must be treated statistically as an endogenous variable. If we were in the standard simultaneous supply and demand econometric model the researcher could replace all endogenous variables on the right-hand side of an equation with values predicted from a reduced-form equation, which is a regression of each endogenous variable on all exogenous variables in the system. How the researcher addresses econometrically the dual endogeneity of pay and workplace characteristics as workers and firms match in hedonic labor market equilibrium is more restricted than in the supply and demand for homogeneous commodities.

The special econometric complexity is that workers with unusually high desires for pleasant work environments (low zs) given their latent attributes (ε^s) will match with firms that are low cost producers of the job amenity as captured in x^d. Similarly, workers less concerned with a pleasant work environment will tend to match with firms where producing a pleasant work environment is difficult and expensive. The result is that ε^S and x^d are not statistically independent; likewise ε^d and x^S are not statistically independent. The practical econometric implication of how workers and firms match is that in predicting (also known as instrumenting) the values of regressors in the supply schedule the researcher may not be able to use exogenous variables from the demand schedule, and in predicting the values of regressors in the demand schedule the researcher may not be able to use exogenous variables from the supply schedule. Thus, there is limited information available to identify the parameters of the workers' preferences embedded in their supply equations (Equation (3.1)) and limited information available to identify the parameters of firms' costs and technologies embedded in their demand equations (Equations (3.2)), which complicates inferring econometrically how policy affects economic well-being. In a subsequent companion paper we examine the econometric ingenuity used to reveal the properties of the structural equations (Equations (3.1) and (3.2)) that are crucial for issues of policy and economic well-being.

Numerous studies examine the reduced-form relationship between wages and workplace risk. The purpose of our discussion of econometric results on the equilibrium locus is not to review the various studies. Instead it is to give a brief flavor of the some of the issues involved in estimating the hedonic relationship that we have ourselves researched. Readers interested in a more detailed discussion of the international evidence on the hedonic wage equation as it reveals the economics of workplace safety issues should see Viscusi and Aldy (2003).

4

Some Policy Relevant Hedonic Equilibrium Estimates

The value of a statistical life (VSL) plays the central role in regulatory decisions affecting risks to life and health. Economists continue to try to improve the accuracy and concomitant usefulness of benefit assessments by examining whether the typically calculated VSL understates the average benefits of life-saving government regulations and whether the heterogeneity in individual VSLs should influence policy.

4.1 The Canonical Hedonic Wage Regression and Implied VSL

The canonical hedonic wage equation used in the value of statistical life calculations in Kniesner and Viscusi (2005) takes the form:

$$\ln(w_{ijk}) = \alpha_1 \pi_{ijk} + X_{ijk}\gamma + u_{ijk}, \tag{4.1}$$

where for worker i in industry j and occupation k, $\ln(w)$ is the natural logarithm of the hourly wage rate, π is the work-related fatality rate, and X is a vector containing both demographic variables (such as education, race, marital status, and union membership) and job characteristic variables (such as the non-fatal injury risk, possibly wage replacement under workers' compensation insurance, and possibly industry, occupation, or geographic location indicators). Finally, u_{ijk} is an error term that may exhibit conditional heteroskedasticity and within fatality risk autocorrelation, which needs to be reflected in the coefficients' calculated standard errors.

With a fatality risk measure of deaths per 100,000 workers and a work year of 2,000 hours, the value of a statistical life is $\text{VSL} = \alpha \times \exp(\ln(w)) \times 100,000 \times 2,000$. Although the VSL function depends on the values of the right-hand side in Equation (4.1), most commonly considered is the mean VSL.

The fatality risk measure in Equation (4.1) is the fatality rate for the worker's industry-occupation group. Workplace fatality risk is publicly available only by industry. To provide a more precise correspondence between the fatality risk and the worker's job, one can construct the fatality risk using unpublished U.S. Bureau of Labor Statistics data from the Census of Fatal Occupational Injuries (CFOI), which is the most comprehensive inventory available of work-related deaths.[1] The number of fatalities in each industry-occupation cell is the numerator of the fatality risk measure, and the number of employees in the industry-occupation group is the denominator of the fatality risk measure.

By way of additional detail, the regressions in Equation (4.1) also use 720 industry-occupation groups, which are the intersection of 72 two-digit SIC code industries and the 10 one-digit occupation groups. For the 6,238 total work-related deaths in 1997 there were 290 industry occupation cells with no reported fatalities. Because total fatalities were relatively similar from 1992, which was the first year of the CFOI, up through the regression sample year of 1997, Equation (4.1) uses mean fatalities for an industry-occupation cell during 1992–1997 when computing fatality risk. Intertemporally averaging reduces the importance of random changes in fatalities and reduces by two-thirds the number of empty fatality risk cells. In the regression sample data the average fatality risk is 4/100,000 with the lowest risk level 0.6/100,000 and the highest about 25/100,000.

[1] The fatality data used by Kniesner and Viscusi (2005) are available on CD-ROM from the BLS. In calculating fatality risk they follow the procedures in Viscusi (2004), who compares the fatality risk measure to other death risk variables and should be consulted for more details.

In addition to the fatality risk variable just described (Kniesner and Viscusi, 2005) estimated the regression in Equation (4.1) with individual data from the 1997 merged outgoing rotation group of the Current Population Survey. Sample individuals are non-agricultural full-time workers (usual weekly hours worked at least 35) between the ages of 18 and 65. The VSL from their baseline regression (Equation (4.1)) is \$4.7 million–\$4.8 million.

4.2 Relative Economic Position and VSL

Some have hypothesized that workers' expected utility depends not only on their job risk and absolute wage, but also on their relative position within the wage distribution (Frank and Sunstein, 2001). Equilibrium market outcomes will then reflect workers' concerns with relative position too. If compensating differentials for risk raise workers' income and relative economic position matters a worker might be willing to accept a lower compensating differential for a given risk than if there were no such relative position effects. The consequence for the computation and application of VSL estimates is that standard VSL estimates are too low because relative position is an omitted variable in the typical hedonic wage equation.

An amended canonical model to include relative position effects is:

$$\ln(w_{ijk}) = \alpha_2 \pi_{jk} + X_{ijk}\gamma + \phi R_i + u_{ijk}, \tag{4.2}$$

where R is the individual's relative position in the wage distribution of some reference group. Equation (4.1) is the possibly mis-specified model, and Equation (4.2) may be the correctly specified model. If Frank and Sunstein are correct, a worker will accept a smaller compensating differential for risk to boost the worker's relevant relative wage, so that $\alpha_2 > \alpha_1 \Rightarrow \mathrm{VSL}(\alpha_2) > \mathrm{VSL}(\alpha_1)$. Ignoring relative position may undervalue safety-enhancing government regulations that do not disturb relative wages, which are properly measured by $\mathrm{VSL}(\alpha_2)$ compared to regulations that alter relative wages, as measured by $\mathrm{VSL}(\alpha_1)$.

Kniesner and Viscusi (2003) offer a lengthy conceptual criticism of the importance of relative position including that it is unlikely a regulation could ever have no distribution effects. Even if relative position effects exist, they seem likely to be small. A worker facing the average fatality risk of 4/100,000 and with the VSL of $4.74 million from estimated (Equation (4.1)) will receive annual fatality risk compensation of $190, which is unlikely to confer substantial economic status. Moreover, if the relative position reference group is defined within firms, to the extent that the riskiest jobs are viewed as unattractive low-prestige positions, this may overshadow any income-based status effect. Thus, even if relative status matters, it is not clear whether the key dimensionality of status derives from wages, which may be unobservable, or the physical attributes of one's job, which are more readily observable.

A practical problem with including a relative position effect based on relative income status is that there is no unique way to infer from the regression what the person's reference group might be.[2] The researcher must start ex ante with the reference group when formulating the regression to estimate and then infer the effects of the possibly incorrect reference group's behavior on the individual's behavior. There is also no evidence from micro surveys to rely on that establishes the typical worker's economic reference group.

Let us consider some potential reference groups to see if group effects when implemented in a regression framework enlarge the VSL. Consider as possible omitted regressors in the canonical model in Equation (4.1) the relative position (percentile rank) of a person's wage in the state of residence and the relative position of a person's wage among persons of the same gender in the state of residence.[3] Kniesner and Viscusi (2005) construct the relative position variable such that the highest

[2] Suppose that my true reference group is only my neighbor in the house to the east, which in the absence of detailed survey data the researcher will not know. A regression model of spatial behavior connections will imply that all the houses on my block are a reference group because within-neighborhood incomes are positively correlated. For more discussion of the impossibility of pinning down the reference group because of geographic and economic nesting of correlated subgroup variables, see Moffitt (2001).

[3] The larger the reference group the closer relative position is to a simple ordinal transformation of the dependent variable, and the smaller the reference group the less informative is the measure of relative position. The state level seems to strike the best balance among possible reference groups. Kniesner and Viscusi tried several reference group alternatives, including age-education as suggested in Woittiez and Kapteyn (1998), and no other reference group rankings yielded significant regression coefficients in Equation (4.2).

wage person has the lowest wage rank variable score, or $R = 1 =$ first is best, and $R =$ group size $=$ last is worst. Their results, demonstrating the effect of adding relative position to a hedonic wage regression, are opposite of Frank and Sunstein's conjecture. Their estimated VSL is about 25–33 percent smaller when relative position is held constant compared to when relative position is ignored.

It is well-known that the change in the coefficient of a linear regression due to adding a variable depends on the product of two things: (1) the partial effect of the new variable and (2) the partial relationship between the originally included variable and the newly included variable, holding constant the other regressors (Greene, 2008, p. 134). Thus, $\alpha_1 > \alpha_2 \Leftrightarrow \phi \times (\partial\pi/\partial R|X) > 0$. In the estimates of Equation (4.2) $\phi < 0$, which simply reflects that relatively high-wage workers also have high absolute wages (remember that $R = 1$ is the highest wage rank). Many persons with relatively high wages in their state also live in higher average fatality rate states, so that $(\partial\pi/\partial R|X) < 0$. Because both terms in the product that determines the change in the coefficient of fatal injury risk are negative, VSL shrinks when relative position is added as a regressor. As least for the measures of relative position one can easily consider, using conventionally computed estimates of VSL based on the canonical hedonic wage regression ignoring relative position do not undervalue possible safety-enhancing government regulations.

4.3 Consumption and VSL

Kniesner et al. (2006) consider in detail the fact that VSL should be computed in light of the worker's consumption plans over the life cycle. Someone with a given life expectancy will have a higher VSL if he or she has back loaded planned consumption than an otherwise identical person whose planned consumption has already occurred (Shepard and Zeckhauser, 1984; Johansson, 2002a,b). Adding consumption plans to a model of the worker's behavior is also a natural way to capture most completely the effects of aging on VSL, which need not be monotonic with age if consumption is sufficiently increasing or non-monotonic with age.

A hedonic model that adds consumption to the canonical model of wages in Equation (4.1) is:

$$\ln(w_{ijk}) = \alpha_3\pi_{ijk} + X_{ijk}\gamma + \delta C_i + u_{ijk}, \qquad (4.3)$$

where C is a measure of the individual's consumption. Because persons with higher intended consumption should also have higher paying jobs, one expects $\delta > 0$ in Equation (4.3). If persons with more planned consumption are wealthier and choose safer jobs, ceteris paribus, C and π conditionally covary negatively $(\partial\pi/\partial C|X < 0)$. According to the formula we discussed earlier for how adding a variable will change the coefficient of π, it should be the case that $\alpha_3 > \alpha_1 \Rightarrow \text{VSL}(\alpha_3) > \text{VSL}(\alpha_1)$, and a model that includes consumption effects has a higher implied value of a statistical life for older workers than if the researcher ignores planned consumption.

The CPS cross-sectional data Kniesner and Viscusi (2005) use do not include data on consumption. Examining the change in VSL from adding consumption requires using a second source of data on individual labor market participants. Kniesner et al. (2006) used the 1997 wave of the Panel Study of Income Dynamics, which also provides individual-level data on wages, consumption, industry and occupation, and demographics.

Concerning consumption, the PSID records food expenditures (inclusive of food stamps) both inside and outside the home and housing expenditures including rent or mortgage payments where applicable. One measure of C use in Equation (4.3) is what the PSID makes readily available, which is the sum of food and housing expenditures. Kniesner et al. (2006) also used imputed total consumption as disposable income net of saving (Ziliak, 1998).

Because consumption is a choice variable they allowed for $\text{E}[u_{ijk}C_i] \neq 0$, which implies the need for an instrumental variables approach to produce a consistent estimate of α_3, the estimated fatality effect in model (Equation (4.3)), to use in calculating VSL. Although choosing an instrument set is always key in IV models, one can rely on relatively standard information from economic theory of individual behavior over the life cycle. Based on human capital theory they take the worker's non-wage income as having no direct effect on the log of the wage, and based on the theory of the consumer take non-wage income as determining consumption.

Kniesner et al. estimates take care of consumption endogeneity by instrumenting with non-wage income as the identifying regressor.[4] The result of interest is that including consumption raises the coefficient of π and its P-value. Adding consumption to the canonical hedonic wage model raises the average VSL by as much as 20 percent.

4.4 Implications of VSL Estimates with Relative Position and Consumption

Relative position is a potentially interesting independent variable because it is a simple way to introduce distributional concerns into cost-effectiveness calculations. VSL computed from a hedonic wage regression with relative economic position as a regressor holds constant a measure of the distributional consequences of a regulation that changes fatality risk. Holding relative economic position constant could allow the analyst to avoid having to address issues of distribution more generally, which can prove highly controversial or lead to strategic manipulation of cost-effectiveness calculations (Sunstein, 2004; Kniesner and Viscusi, 2003, 2005). However, the level of VSL is the main effect of interest, and introducing relative wage position into the canonical hedonic regression if anything lowers, not raises, VSL. The main policy implication of the results concerning relative position is that, as typically computed, VSL is not undervalued by ignoring a worker's relative position in the wage distribution.

The conclusion and ultimate policy implication are reversed when one considers that worker's wages are jointly determined with consumption plans. The consequence is that VSL is explicitly a function of the individual's consumption. We have demonstrated that consumption is a significant additional variable in hedonic models used to produce,

[4] Other independent variables in the first-stage IV regression for consumption are a quadratic in age, fatality risk, education, race, marital status, union status, one-digit occupation, and region of residence. Non-labor income is statistically significant at the 0.01 level and $R^2 = 0.3$.

VSL and that incorporating consumption raises VSL by as much as 20 percent, most notably for middle-aged and older workers.

If one wants to net out distributional consequences of policies that affect mortality risk the most transparent way, looking at the effect of policy for workers of a given wealth level could be the best approach. Because consumption changes with age, models that include consumption are a natural way to infer how VSL changes with age, which need not be monotonic if workers have back loaded their planned consumption (Kniesner et al., 2006).

4.5 Panel Data and Additive Unobserved Heterogeneity

Notwithstanding the wide use of the VSL approach, there is still concern over excessively large/small estimates and the wide range of VSL estimates. The wide range of estimates occur for a variety of reasons. Samples and risk characteristics of the samples vary among studies. At least in the United States, union members have higher VSLs than non-union workers (Viscusi and Aldy, 2003); whites have higher VSLs than blacks (Viscusi, 2003); and women have higher, but more statistically fragile, VSLs than men (Leeth and Ruser, 2003). VSLs for native workers are roughly the same as for immigrant workers, except for non-English-speaking immigrants from Mexico who appear to earn little compensation for bearing very high levels of workplace risk (Viscusi and Hersch, 2010). VSLs vary by age with values rising until the mid-40s and then very gradually falling (Kniesner et al., 2006; Aldy and Viscusi, 2008). And a substantial body of research discovers a very strong positive relationship between income and VSLs (Viscusi, 2009). The crux of all the studies is that there is not a single, immutable VSL. Risk preferences, knowledge, safety productivity, income, and/or discrimination result in differences across countries, over time, or across demographic groups and policy makers wishing to use estimated VSLs for cost/benefit analyses must be careful to choose a value appropriate for the group affected by the change in safety policy.

VSL estimates also vary by how risk is measured. Many of the risk measures used in the early VSL studies now appear to be relatively unreliable. Initial studies often used BLS fatal injury rate statistics at the two-digit and three-digit industry levels, which were generated using a sampling of companies. The relative infrequency of workplace fatalities causes the BLS statistics to be subject to considerable measurement error. Other VSL studies used data released by the Society of Actuaries, detailing the added risk of death from working in 37 very high-risk occupations. The Society of Actuaries data likely overstate the true frequency of injury because the data cover only very hazardous occupations and because people who choose high-risk occupations may also accept greater risk off the job. A few other researchers used workers' compensation data to generate measures of risk or relied on data released by the National Institute of Occupational Safety and Health detailing workplace fatalities by one-digit industry and state.

In 1992, the BLS began releasing fatal injury rate data through the Census of Fatal Occupational Injuries (CFOI). The BLS determines work relatedness by examining death certificates, medical examiner reports, OSHA reports, and workers' compensation records. The new data on fatalities are much more reliable than the previous data. The underlying data also contain information on worker characteristics such as gender, race/nationality, age, and immigrant status, job characteristics such as occupation and industry, and the circumstance underlying the event, allowing researchers to calculate fatality rates much more narrowly tailored to the population under investigation, again raising the reliability of the new VSL estimates.

One approach to dealing with the dispersion of VSL estimates, which has been used by the U.S. Environmental Protection Agency, has been to rely on meta-analyses of the labor market VSL literature. The difficulty with meta-analyses is that they include results from studies with known problems, which "imparts biases of unknown magnitude and direction," (Viscusi, 2009, p. 118). Kniesner et al. (2010a) take another approach and demonstrate how using the best available data and econometric practices affects the estimated VSL so as to narrow the range of estimates.

They begin with an econometric framework that is a slight extension of the usual hedonic wage equation used in the value of statistical life literature. For worker $i (i = 1, \ldots, N)$ in industry $j (j = 1, \ldots, J)$ and occupation $k (k = 1, \ldots, K)$ at time $t (t = 1, \ldots, T)$ the hedonic tradeoff between the wage and risk of fatality is described by:

$$\ln(w_{ijkt}) = \alpha_{0i}^{+} + \alpha_{0i}^{-} + \alpha_1 \pi_{jkt} + X_{ijkt}\beta + u_{ijkt}, \qquad (4.4)$$

where $\ln(w_{ijkt})$ is the natural log of the hourly wage rate; π_{jkt} is the industry and occupation specific fatality rate; X_{ijkt} is a vector containing dummy variables for the worker's one-digit occupation (and industry in some specifications), state and region of residence, plus the usual demographic variables: worker education, age and age squared, race, marital status, and union status; u_{ijkt} is an error term allowing conditional heteroskedasticity and within industry by occupation autocorrelation.[5] Equation (4.4) is slightly unfamiliar as it contains two latent individual effects: one that is positively correlated with wages and the fatality rate (α_{0i}^{+}) and one that is positively correlated with wages and negatively correlated with the fatality rate (α_{0i}^{-}). The first individual effect reflects unmeasured job productivity that leads more productive/higher wage workers to take safer jobs and the second individual effect reflects unmeasured individual differences in personal safety productivity that leads higher wage workers to take what appears to be more dangerous jobs because the true danger level for such a worker is lower than the measured fatality rate. Their research uses Equation (4.4) in conjunction with a variety of econometric techniques, which demonstrates the capabilities of individual panel data that incorporate fatality risk measures that vary by year.

Kniesner et al. devote particular attention to measurement errors, which have been noted in Black and Kniesner (2003), Ashenfelter and Greenstone (2004), and Ashenfelter (2006). Although they do not have information on subjective risk beliefs, they use very detailed data on objective risk measures and consider the possibility that workers are driven by risk expectations. Published industry risk beliefs are strongly correlated with subjective risk values,[6] and they follow the standard practice of matching to workers in the sample an objective risk measure.

[5] Kniesner et al. (2010a) adopt a parametric specification of the regression model representing hedonic equilibrium in Equation (4.4) for comparison purposes with the existing literature. An important emerging line of research is how more econometrically free-form representations of hedonic labor markets facilitates identification of underlying fundamentals, which would further generalize estimates of VSL (Ekeland et al., 2004).

[6] See Viscusi and Aldy (2003) for a review.

Where Kniesner et al. (2010a) differ from most previous studies is the pertinence of the risk data to the worker's particular job, and theirs is the first study to account for the variation of the more pertinent risk level within the context of a panel data study. Their work also distinguishes job movers from job stayers. They find that most of the variation in risk and most of the evidence of positive VSLs stem from people changing jobs across occupations or industries possibly endogenously rather than from variation in risk levels over time in a given job setting.

Their econometric refinements using panel data have a substantial effect on the estimated VSL levels. They reduce the estimated VSL by more than 50 percent from the implausibly large cross-section PSID-based VSLs of \$20 million–\$30 million. They demonstrate how systematic econometric modeling narrows the estimated value of a statistical life from about \$0 million–\$30 million to about \$7 million–\$12 million, which Kniesner et al. (2010a) then show clarifies the choice of the proper labor market-based VSL for policy evaluations.

4.5.1 More Details on Linear Panel Data Econometric Models

Standard panel-data estimators permitting latent worker-specific heterogeneity through person-specific intercepts in Equation (4.4) are the deviation from time-mean (within) estimator and the time-difference (first- and long-differences) estimators. The fixed effects include all person-specific time-invariant differences in tastes and all aspects of productivity, which may be correlated with the regressors in X. The two estimators yield identical results when there are two time periods and when the number of periods converges toward infinity. With a finite number of periods ($T > 2$), estimates from the two different fixed-effects estimators can diverge due to possible non-stationarity in wages, measurement error, or model misspecification (Wooldridge, 2002). Because wages from longitudinal data on individuals have been shown to be non-stationary in other contexts (Abowd and Card, 1989; MaCurdy, 2007), Kniesner et al. adopt the first-difference model as a baseline.

The first-difference model eliminates time-invariant effects by estimating the changes over time in hedonic equilibrium:

$$\Delta \ln(w_{ijkt}) = \alpha_1 \Delta \pi_{jkt} + \Delta X_{ijkt}\beta + \Delta u_{ijkt}, \tag{4.5}$$

where Δ refers to the first-difference operator (Weiss and Lillard, 1978).

The first-difference model could exacerbate errors-in-variables problems relative to the within model (Griliches and Hausman, 1986). If the fatality rate is measured with a classical error, then the first-difference estimate of $\hat{\alpha}_1$ may be attenuated relative to the within estimate. An advantage of the regression specification in Equation (4.5), which considers intertemporal changes in hedonic equilibrium outcomes, arises because one can use so-called wider (2+ year) differences. If $\Delta \geq 2$ then measurement error effects are mitigated in Equation (4.5) relative to within-differences regression (Griliches and Hausman, 1986; Hahn et al., 2007). As discussed in the data section below, Kniesner et al. additionally address the measurement error issue in the fatality rate by employing multi-year averages of fatalities. For completeness we note how the first-difference and longer-differences estimates compare to the within estimates.

Lillard and Weiss (1979) demonstrated that earnings functions may not only have idiosyncratic differences in levels but also have idiosyncratic differences in growth. To correct for wages that may not be difference stationary as implied by Equation (4.5) they estimate a double differenced version of Equation (4.5) that is:

$$\Delta^2 \ln(w_{ijkt}) = \alpha_1 \Delta^2 \pi_{jkt} + \Delta^2 X_{ijkt}\beta + \Delta^2 u_{ijkt}, \tag{4.6}$$

where $\Delta^2 = \Delta_t - \Delta_{t-1}$, commonly known as the difference-in-difference operator.

Finally, Kniesner et al. estimate a dynamic version of Equation (4.6) by adding $\gamma \Delta \ln(w_{ijkt-1})$ to the right-hand side and using two first-difference instrumental variables estimators: (i) using the two-period lagged level of the dependent variable as an identifying instrument for the one-period lagged difference in the dependent variable (Greene, 2008, Chapter 15) and (ii) using an instrument set that grows as the time-series dimension of the panel evolves (Arellano and Bond, 1991). The lagged dependent variable controls for additional heterogeneity and serial correlation plus sluggish adjustment to equilibrium (state dependence). One can then compare the estimated short-run effect, $\hat{\alpha}_1$, with the estimated long-run effect, $\hat{\alpha}_1/(1-\hat{\gamma})$, and their associated VSLs.

4.5.2 Focal Estimates from Panel Data

The VSL implied by a baseline model's coefficient for the annual fatality rate (Equation (4.4)) using the sample mean wage of $21 is $6.9 million, with a confidence interval of $6.8 million–$7.1 million.[7] Compared to VSL from the more typical annual risk measure, the estimated VSL is about 13 percent larger when fatality risk is a three-year average. Results for the widest possible differences, which is for $(\ln(w_{2001}) - \ln(w_{1993}))$ as well as difference-in-differences from Equation (4.6), which should remove possible spurious estimated effects from variables that are not difference stationary. An important message is that correcting for measurement error in most cases enlarges estimated VSL, and that even for the relatively basic panel models using differencing, the range for VSL is not uncomfortably large: about $7 million–$9 million when using a 2,000-hour work year (CI = $6.8 million–$9.7 million) and about $8 million–$10 million when using sample average hours to compute VSL (CI = $7.5 million–$10.9 million).

An issue seldom addressed in panel wage equations producing VSL is endogeneity of the fatality change regressor, which may result from dynamic decisions workers make to change jobs (Solon, 1986, 1989; Spengler and Schaffner, 2006). Some changes in fatality risk will occur because of within industry-occupation cell changes and others will occur because workers switch industry-occupation cells. Where there is potentially hazardous employment, much of the mobility stems from workers learning about the risks on the job and then quitting if the compensating differential is insufficient given that information (Viscusi, 1979). Within the context of multi-period Bayesian decisions, a desire to switch does not require that workers initially underestimated the risk, as imprecise risk beliefs can also generate a greater willingness

[7] The confidence interval uses a first-order Taylor series expansion to estimate the variance of the mean *VSL*, which from Equation (4.4) is $Var(\overline{VSL}) = 2{,}000^2 * 100{,}000^2 * (\bar{w}^2 * Var(\hat{\alpha}_1) + \hat{\alpha}_1^2 Var(\bar{w}))$.

to incur job risks than is warranted by the mean risk level. For the job changers in the Kniesner et al. sample, 51 percent switch to lower fatality risk jobs and 46 percent switch to higher fatality risk jobs so that on balance there is some effort to sort into safer employment.

Kniesner et al. therefore examine the practical importance of job changing status for panel-based estimation by stratifying the data by whether $\Delta\pi_t$ is due to within or between cell changes, including immediately before and after a worker changes cells. The main econometric contribution to compensating differentials for fatality risk comes from workers who generate differences in risk over time by switching industry-occupation cells. The difference in estimated VSL comes from the fact that $\sigma^2_{\pi_t}$ is at least eight times larger for switchers. There is too little within-cells variation to reveal much of a compensating differential for job stayers. More important, because so much of the variation producing the wage differential comes from job changers, and the variation for switchers may be related to wages, it is imperative to treat $\Delta\pi$ as endogenous.

The estimated range for VSL narrows even further when Kniesner et al. allow for endogeneity and instrument the change in fatality risk. Their instrumental variables regressions control for both classical measurement errors and endogeneity. Specifically, based on the results of Griliches and Hausman (1986) they interchangeably use the $(t-1)$ and $(t-3)$ levels of the fatality risk, or the $[(t-1)-(t-3)]$ difference. They limit the focus to the annual fatality rate so as to have enough lagged fatality and fatality differences as instruments.[8] The main result is a fairly narrow range for the estimated VSL, approximately \$7 million–\$8 million when Kniesner et al. instrument the annual change in fatality risk (CI = \$6.6–\$8 million).

The first-differences estimator in Equation (4.5) focuses on changes in wages in response to changes in risk. The mechanism by which the changes will become reflected in the labor market hinges on how shifts

[8] Greene (2008, Chapter 15) notes that the large sample variance of the dynamic difference estimator is smaller when lagged levels rather than lagged differences are part of the instruments, which here include all exogenous explanatory variables. The first-stage results here and in subsequent tables pass the standard weak instruments check based on a partial R^2 of at least 0.10.

in the risk level will affect the tangencies of the constant expected utility loci with the market offer curve. To the extent that the updating of risk beliefs occurs gradually over time, which is not unreasonable because even release of the government risk data is not contemporaneous, one would expect the long-run effects on wages of changes in job risk to exceed the short-run effects. Limitations on mobility will reinforce a lagged influence (state dependence).

As one would then expect, the steady-state estimates of VSL after the estimated three-year adjustment period are larger than the short-run estimates. The difference between the short-run and long-run VSL is about \$2 million, ranging from \$7 million to \$8 million versus \$9 million to \$10 million using a standard work year. The range of VSL estimates is not great when panel data are used with estimators that accommodate endogeneity, weak instruments, measurement error, latent heterogeneity, and possible state dependence.

4.5.3 Comparison Results from Cross-Section Estimators

One problematic result in the literature is the regularly occurring large value for VSL when the PSID is used as a cross-section (Viscusi and Aldy, 2003). Cross-section estimators produce large implied VSLs, about \$16 million–\$28 million. In contrast, consider estimates from a simple panel random-effects estimator, where a Breusch–Pagan test supports heterogeneous intercepts. Recall that the random-effects estimator accounts for unobserved heterogeneity, which is assumed to be uncorrelated with observed covariates. It is fairly common in labor market research to reject the assumption of no correlation between unobserved heterogeneity and observed covariates; and Hausman test results indicate a similar rejection in the Kniesner et al. results. The simple fixed effects within estimator is preferred over the simple random-effects estimator, with an estimated VSL of about \$6 million–\$8 million. Allowing for the possibility of unobserved productivity and preferences for risk, even if it is improperly assumed to be randomly distributed in the population, reduces the estimated VSL by up to 60 percent relative to a model that ignores latent heterogeneity.

The difference in estimated VSL with versus without latent individual heterogeneity in the model is consistent with the theoretical emphasis in Shogren and Stamland (2002) that failure to control for unobserved skill results in a potentially substantial upward bias in the estimated VSL. Taking into account the influence of individual heterogeneity implies that, on balance, unobservable person-specific differences in safety-related productivity and risk preferences are a more powerful influence than unobservable productivity generally, which Hwang et al. (1992) hypothesize to have the opposite effect.

4.5.4 Implications for Regulatory Cost-Effectiveness

The wide variation of VSL estimates in the literature has generated concern that underlying econometric problems may jeopardize the validity of the estimates. The range for VSL in the existing literature is extremely wide, from about \$0 million to \$20 million. Cross-section data studies using the Panel Study of Income Dynamics have often yielded extremely high VSL estimates of \$20+ million. A most important finding from Kniesner et al. is that controlling for latent time-invariant heterogeneity is crucial — much more so than how one does it econometrically.

Their first-difference estimation results use more refined fatality risk measures than employed in earlier studies control for measurement errors and workplace safety endogeneity in econometric specifications considering state dependence, expectations, and heterogeneity when examining the wage-fatality risk tradeoff. Comparison of the various first-difference results with various cross-section estimates implies that controlling for latent worker-specific heterogeneity reduces the estimated VSL by as much as two-thirds and narrows greatly the VSL range to about \$7 million–\$12 million depending on the time-frame (short-run versus long-run).

Narrowing VSL as they do has substantial benefits for policy evaluation in that it narrows the uncertainty concerning cost-effective programs. As a specific example, in its Budget Circular A4 (September 17, 2003), the U.S. Office of Management and Budget requires that agencies indicate the range of uncertainty around key parameter values used in benefit–cost assessments. Attempting to bound the VSL based on a meta-analysis produces a wide range of estimates from nearly \$0 to \$20+ million. In addition to the issue of what studies should be included in the meta-analysis given the differences in data sets, specifications, and study quality, we can also produce VSLs that mimic the literature with ones as low as \$0 if one limits the sample to workers who never change jobs and ones as high as \$28 million if one uses the between estimator with the PSID as a cross-section (CI = −\$5.4 million to \$28.1 million). Because of the perceived indeterminacies in VSL, agencies often have failed to provide any boundaries at all to the key VSL parameter in their benefit assessments.

The advantage of using the Kniesner et al. VSL range in policy assessments can be illustrated by an example of the cost-effectiveness of U.S. health and safety regulations. Using the widely cited cost estimates from the U.S. Office of Management and Budget cited by Breyer (1993), among others, and updating the values to \$2001 to be consistent with their VSL estimates, we illustrate the reduction of policy uncertainty achievable by application of the Kniesner et al. estimates. Applying the meta-analysis VSL range, 10 policies pass a benefit–cost test, 20 fail a benefit–cost test, and 23 are in the indeterminate zone. Using the Kniesner et al. estimated VSL range, the distribution becomes 27 policies that clearly pass a benefit–cost test, 23 that fail a benefit–cost test, with only 3 policies in the indeterminate range, which is described in Figure 4.1. The narrowing of the acceptable cost-per-life-saved range greatly reduces the range of indeterminacy and is of substantial practical consequence given the actual distribution of regulatory policy performance.

4.6 A Deeper Look at Policy Relevant Heterogeneity: Panel Data Quantile Regression

We have seen that there are many sources of heterogeneity in hedonic wage equations, both latent and those stemming from age and other demographic factors. Recent research by Kniesner et al. (2010b) examines the economic and policy importance of heterogeneity in VSL based on income and the closely related matter of the person's risk-taking behavior and needed compensation for additional risk.

In particular, they examine the VSL distribution across the population using quantile regression estimates from panel data on workers'

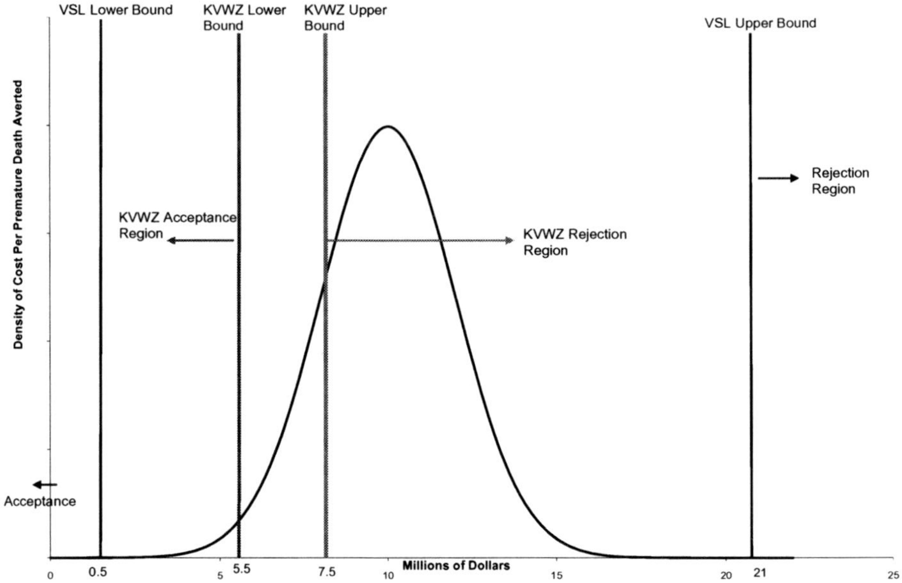

Fig. 4.1 Narrowing the range of acceptable programs.

wages, which yields estimates of the VSL for different segments of the wage distribution that are associated with different fatality risk levels and income levels. Because safety is a normal good, workers with higher income levels will have higher VSL levels and will tend to choose jobs with lower risk levels. Their empirical research explores the heterogeneity of VSL across different segments of the wage distribution and the associated income levels of people in the segments to infer the income elasticity of VSL. The resulting evidence on the relationship of VSL to income levels and to fatality risk levels have been matters of policy concern.

The counterpart of the risk–VSL relationship is the risk–income relationship. The U.S. Department of Transportation (DOT) provides for consideration of income in setting the VSL for benefit assessment, as it permits the use of an income elasticity adjustment of 0.55 based on the meta-analysis of Viscusi and Aldy (2003).[9] Agencies within DOT,

[9] U.S. Department of Transportation, Office of the Assistant Secretary for Transportation Policy, Revised Departmental Guidance: Treatment of the Value of Preventing Fatalities and Injuries in Preparing Economic Analyses, August 2, 2005.

notably the Federal Aviation Administration, have long maintained that the higher income levels of those protected by their regulations imply that a higher VSL level should be used for their regulations than for transportation policies generally.[10] Senate Bill S. 3564 also recognized the role of income adjustments, stating that the VSL amount must be increased annually to reflect changes in income.[11] The proposed legislation did not permit decreasing VSL if income levels decline, which incomes did during the recession that began shortly after the legislation was proposed in 2008. The estimates from Kniesner et al. (2010b) indicate whether an income-based adjustment to VSL is warranted and to what extent.

In a quantile wage regression the VSLs vary with the potential wage ($\hat{w}$), which admits the possibility that VSL varies positively with income levels and permits the calculation of income elasticities for the different quantile groups. When income elasticities of VSL differ by income levels, it opens the door for Ramsey pricing of safety programs similar to that used for other health-related programs such as hospital pricing, where the decision is health with distributional consequences (Harris, 1979).

Estimates of the income elasticity are also useful in exploring whether the model underlying the hedonic equilibrium equation yields results consistent with economic theory. Kaplow (2005), among others, has noted the connection between risk aversion and VSL and has emphasized that VSL must be income elastic for the empirical results to be consistent with estimates based on the estimated coefficient of relative risk aversion in the consumption literature. Based on existing estimates in the literature, there is currently a disconnect between the theory and empirical evidence. The VSL has an estimated income elasticity less than 1.0, whereas risk aversion estimates would imply a VSL

---

[10] Graham (2008) suggests that when policies have clearly different target groups, such as air travel versus bus travel, then income elasticities might be taken into account.Similarly, the Federal Aviation Administration sought to use a higher value of life than for other transportation policies because of the higher income of air travelers. See Viscusi (1993), which is based on his report to the FAA that the agency sought to use in justifying use of a higher VSL.

[11] More specifically, VSL must be increased at least once a year to reflect "the average annual total compensation of individuals, including income and benefits."

that is income elastic (Kniesner and Ziliak, 2002; Viscusi and Aldy, 2003; Aldy and Viscusi, 2008). The Kniesner et al. (2010b) income elasticity estimates establish the consistency between the risk preferences and VSL literatures that have eluded economists to now.

The potential variation of the VSL with wage levels also has implications for the relation of VSL to risk levels. Consider a standard hedonic wage model. For any given firm, the offer curve of wages for different levels of risk will be governed by the requirements that workers be paid their marginal product and profits equal zero. Because safety is costly to provide, and increasingly so as the level of safety is increased, the wage offer curve $w(\pi)$ for the firm as a function of the risk level π will satisfy $dw/d\pi > 0$ and $d^2w/d\pi^2 < 0$. The market offer curve $W(\pi)$ is the outer envelope of the individual firms' offer curves and is generally assumed to have similar shape with $dW/d\pi > 0$ and $d^2W/d\pi^2 < 0$.[12] Workers choose various points along the market offer curve, with the local rate of tradeoff simultaneously reflecting the wage–risk tradeoff along the worker's constant expected utility locus and the wage–risk tradeoff on the firm's isoprofit curve.

The hedonic labor market equation $W(\pi)$ estimates the locus of such choices. If all workers choose the same job, individual preferences would be determining the market tradeoff rate rather than the curvature of the market opportunities locus. But with people sorted along different points of the opportunities locus the shape of the opportunities will be influential. Four empirical studies have examined the curvature of the market equilibrium wage–risk tradeoffs.[13] Each of the studies found that a worker's wages are positively related to the level of risk, but at a diminishing rate. Thus, the VSL varies with the level of risk and declines as the risk level increases, as workers most willing to bear risk sort themselves into the riskiest pursuits. The VSL–risk relationship is also consistent with the hypothesized theoretical shape of the market opportunities locus. Quantile regression analysis estimates the VSL levels at different junctures of the wage offer curve, generating

[12] Should there be any downward dip in the market offer curve, no worker would ever choose such a job that is dominated by available jobs offering higher wage for lower risk.

[13] The studies, which are reviewed in Viscusi and Aldy (2003), are Viscusi (1981), Olson (1981), Dorsey and Walzer (1983), and Leigh and Folsom (1984).

information on the relationship of VSL to the fatality risk and worker income levels.

4.6.1 The Quantile Regression Framework

In the previous section we saw that individual heterogeneity in the form of a latent time-invariant intercept is crucially important to estimating VSL in a linear panel data regression model, much more so than endogeneity of fatal injury risk (Kniesner et al., 2010b). It was also the case that how one controlled for heterogeneity (fixed effects versus a misspecified exogenous random effects model) was far less important to the estimates than whether one controls for differential intercepts at all.

Now we consider slope differences using the concept of quantile regression. It is only recently that estimators have appeared for quantile regression in a panel context that also permit latent person-specific heterogeneity (Koenker, 2004; Lamarche, 2010). Interquartile differences in estimated fatality risk marginal effects and the associated VSLs capture distributional issues such as asymmetry not evident in mean regression. Even a simple comparison of the mean with median VSL is instructive for safety policy where the VSL is a benefit comparison point for evaluating life-saving programs with different cost levels. In particular, using the median program benefit as a cutoff value ensures that a majority of the affected population will benefit from the program, which need not be the case using the mean of an asymmetric benefit distribution as a cost-effectiveness cutoff.

To fix notation consider a general algebraic representation of a hedonic wage equation:

$$\ln(w_{it}) = x_{it}' \, \beta + \alpha_i + u_{it}, \tag{4.7}$$

where i indexes the worker, t indexes time, and the vector of covariates (x) includes fatal injury risk (π) and the usual demographic characteristics of the worker. The α_is are the time-invariant worker-specific effects, and u_{it} is the usual random error term. In Equation (4.7) there are common marginal effects.

In a quantile regression model one has $\beta(\tau_j)$ where τ_j indexes the quantiles of the potential regression outcomes. For tractability, when T

is finite the researcher usually begins by assuming that the worker-specific effect, α_i, is a so-called pure location shift that applies (is common) to all the conditional quantiles of the regression outcomes. Kniesner et al. (2010b) follow the innovative regression model developed in Lamarche (2010). He begins by noting that a shrinkage estimator wherein a tuning parameter (call it λ) controls the degree of inter-person intercept differences is a way to limit the variability of the multiplicity of marginal effect estimates in a quantile regression. The tuning parameter ranges across the spectrum of complete to no heterogeneity and can either be estimated or fixed ex ante. The idea is the optimal shrinkage of the differentials toward a common intercept. They minimize the trace of the covariance matrix when estimating the tuning parameter as well as provide estimates of several extreme cases, such as complete versus no intercept heterogeneity.

Specifically, Lamarche's (2010) estimator finds the

$$\arg\min(\beta,\alpha)\sum_{j=1}^{J}\sum_{t=1}^{T}\sum_{i=1}^{N}\omega_{\tau_j}\rho_{\tau_j}(\ln(w_{it}) - x'_{it}\beta(\tau_j) - \alpha_i) + \lambda\sum_{i=1}^{N}|\alpha_i|, \tag{4.8}$$

where ω_{τ_j} is the relative weight of the j-th quantile and $\rho_{\tau_j}(u) = u(\tau_j - I(u \leq 0))$ is the quantile loss function.

Here the tuning parameter ($\lambda = \sigma_u^2/\sigma_\alpha^2$) regulates the influence on the quantiles of the estimated worker effects. In the case where $\lambda = 0$ the fixed-effects estimator emerges while for the case where $\lambda > 0$ a penalized (shrinkage) estimator with fixed effects appears (Lamarche, 2010). Kniesner et al. (2010b) explore two ways of valuing λ, fixing it ex ante, as the estimator $\hat{\beta}(\tau,\lambda)$ is asymptotically unbiased for all $\lambda > 0$, and finding its trace minimizing estimated value, which is a form of feasible generalized least squares (GLS) analogous to penalized least squares for panel data (Lamarche, 2010). Finally, the pattern of $\hat{\beta}(\tau_j)$ describes how the resulting marginal impact of fatality risk varies across potential wage outcomes.

Kniesner et al. (2010b) also use their estimates of $\hat{\beta}_1(\tau_j)$ to construct estimates of the value of a statistical life and note how the associated VSLs vary across potential wage outcomes. Accounting for the fact that fatality risk is per 100,000 workers and that the typical work year is about 2,000 hours, the estimated value of a statistical life for a quantile of the potential wage distribution is:

$$VSL(\tau_j) = \left[\left(\frac{\partial \hat{w}}{\partial \pi}(\tau_j) = \hat{\beta}_1(\tau_j) \times w(\tau_j) \right) \times 2,000 \times 100,000 \right]. \quad (4.9)$$

To summarize, Equations (4.7) and (4.9) describe the organizing framework: Equation (4.7) is the hedonic market wage locus and Equation (4.9) is the associated value of statistical life (VSL), which depends on the *estimated* parameters of Equation (4.7) via the marginal effect of fatal injury risk (π) and is non-constant in the context of a quantile regression estimator (Equation (4.8)). There are two kinds of heterogeneity that come into play. One is econometric heterogeneity whereby the wage equation intercepts vary with the person indicator (i). The other is economic heterogeneity whereby there is curvature of the hedonic locus ($\hat{\beta}$ varies with τ) to reflect both latent worker and firm differences in risk tolerance and cost functions.

4.6.2 Quantile Estimates: Marginal Effects and VSL

In their PSID-based estimates Kniesner et al. (2010b) found that the regression for $\lambda = 1$ minimized the trace of the variance–covariance matrix. As a result, they focus on the estimated marginal effects from the regression selected by the econometric model, which is where $\hat{\lambda} = 1$, and $\hat{\beta}(\tau = 0.90)/\hat{\beta}(\tau = 0.10) = 1.5$. They then present two different calculations of VSL: one uses the quantiles' actual wage rate averages so that the VSL computation using Equation (4.8) reflects inter-quantile differences in both marginal effects and potential wages, and one that standardizes the VSL by the median wage rate. The $VSL(\tau = 0.90)/VSL(\tau = 0.10) \cong 5$ when both sources of variation are included versus $VSL(\tau = 0.90)/VSL(\tau = 0.10) \cong 1.5$ based on differences in marginal effects alone. The effect of the wage in the calculation is much more important than the effect of the differences in estimated marginal effects of fatal injury risk. Of course, in both cases the median VSL is about \$7 million to \$8 million and is a possible cutoff for regulatory policy decisions in that regulations costing no more than this benefit at least half the affected population.

The essence of the quantile regression approach is that the estimated marginal effects differ by potential wage (and therefore income) so that there is (more) nonlinear curvature potential. The policy relevance of their results includes how they may pertain to updating of the VSL for income growth when used in regulatory agency decisions. The implication of how the curvature is reduced when controlling for individual intercepts is analogous to the issue of poolability in linear panel models. As is well-known, if there is a positive marginal effect of a covariate and intercepts vary positively with the covariate, then an equation that pools the data and forces a common intercept will estimate a steeper regression line than the flatter (set of) true regression lines that have intercept heterogeneity. Analogously, Kniesner et al. (2010b) found that the curvature is reduced dramatically (the marginal effect of fatality is more similar across quantiles) when they allowed for intercept heterogeneity. As in the case of the linear panel models we have estimated in earlier papers, the researcher needs to allow for intercept heterogeneity in panel quantile models of hedonic wage equilibrium with fatal injury risk.

4.6.3 Policy Relevant Heterogeneity: The Income Elasticity of VSL

Quantile estimates of the VSL can be used in conjunction with family income information in the PSID to calculate the income elasticity of the VSL,

$$\eta(\tau_j)_{VSL,y} = (\partial VSL(\tau_j)/\partial y(\tau_j))(y(\tau_j)/VSL(\tau_j)). \tag{4.10}$$

Kniesner et al. (2010b) estimate the elasticity of the estimated VSL at different quantiles with respect to the real family income levels at the quantiles.[14] Based on a linear regression of VSL on the quantile-specific real family income, the overall income elasticity of VSL across the quantiles is 1.44.[15] The elasticity amount varies depending on the

[14] Note that estimates do in fact construct an income elasticity based on real family income levels, whereas what the previous literature refers to as an income elasticity is actually an elasticity with respect to worker wage levels.

[15] The linear equation used to estimate income elasticity is VSL $= -5499606(773449) + 259.3(9.6)$, $R^2 = 0.998$.

quantile, with a high value of 2.24 at the low-wage 0.10 quantile to a low elasticity value of 1.23 at the high-wage 0.90 quantile.[16] The estimates are similar for a specification that also includes a quadratic real family income term, with an overall elasticity of 1.32 and an elasticity range from 2.06 at low wage levels to 1.16 at high wage levels. In each case, higher income levels have the most pronounced effect on the VSL for the low-wage workers, and the elasticity estimates throughout all quantile values are above 1.0.

The very high income elasticity of VSL at low wage levels may account for why countries at less advanced stages of development enact very few health, safety, or environmental regulations until per capita income levels in those countries rise to an adequate level. The perceived economic benefits of risk regulation will be extremely low if income levels are low because the VSL declines at very low income levels at a rate that is more than proportional to the decrease in income.

The Kniesner et al. (2010b) estimates of a large income elasticity of VSL are consistent with the simple theoretical models that have been developed. Kaplow (2005), for example, develops a model of VSL in which there is no bequest motive and the person picks the level of precautionary expenditures.[17] In his model the coefficient of relative risk aversion provides a lower bound on the consumption elasticity of VSL, which is similar to but not identical to the income elasticity. With recent estimates of the coefficient of relative risk aversion being around 2 based on the labor supply analysis of Chetty (2006) and the consumption analysis of Kniesner and Ziliak (2002), one would expect the VSL to be income elastic, which is what the results above indicate.

Kniesner et al. (2010b) find substantial heterogeneity in the marginal effects of fatal injury risk on wages using panel data and a quantile regression model that admits latent intercept heterogeneity. Inter-quantile differences in wages further magnify the differences in VSL so that it varies by a factor of 4.0 in their preferred regression

[16] The quantile ranges are based on the quantile values at points estimated in the regressions. One would expect the elasticity value to be even greater at the 0.01 quantile.

[17] Other studies of this relationship along similar lines include Eeckhoudt and Hammitt (2001) and Evans and Smith (2010). The latter paper shows that with more complex and more realistic models the relationship between the income elasticity of VSL, and the coefficient of relative risk aversion becomes less clear cut.

specification. Although the extreme differences affect the arithmetic mean VSL, it does not affect the median VSL.

The income-elastic VSL Kniesner et al. (2010b) find is important for two reasons, one related to removing a seeming inconsistency in two strands of empirical research and the other related to updating regulatory policy decisions for societal income growth or targeting cutoffs according to the affected population. An income-elastic VSL is required for it to be consistent with the estimated risk aversion parameters in the literature. Even if one does not find it politically feasible to use regulatory cost cutoffs that vary with the incomes of the target population, their results support increasing a common cutoff over time proportionately with society's income growth at a minimum

5

Studying Hedonic Policy Outcomes with Simulations

Because of the extreme data demands of a complete structural hedonic model of the labor market Kniesner and Leeth (1995a,b) consider the alternative of numerical simulation. Instead of trying to use data to identify econometrically firms and workers' value functions they take the research in another direction via numerical simulation or so-called computable hedonic equilibrium.

They begin with evidence from the econometric literature concerning workers' heterogeneous preferences toward risk and firms' heterogeneous costs of making the workplace safer and formulate a computable hedonic model similar to Equations (3.1)–(3.3). In particular, they solve numerically for a set of outcomes that replicates the pre-OSHA labor market in the United States. They then introduce OSHA plus refinements to workers' compensation insurance into the model to compute the new equilibrium that results from workers and firms re-optimizing in the face of a change in the policy regime. A before-and-after numerical comparison then allows them to infer the safety and welfare effects of public policy intended to make workplaces safer and the affected workers economically better off as a result.

Figure 5.1 presents an overview of the numerical model they develop. Their integrated approach to the linkages among the labor,

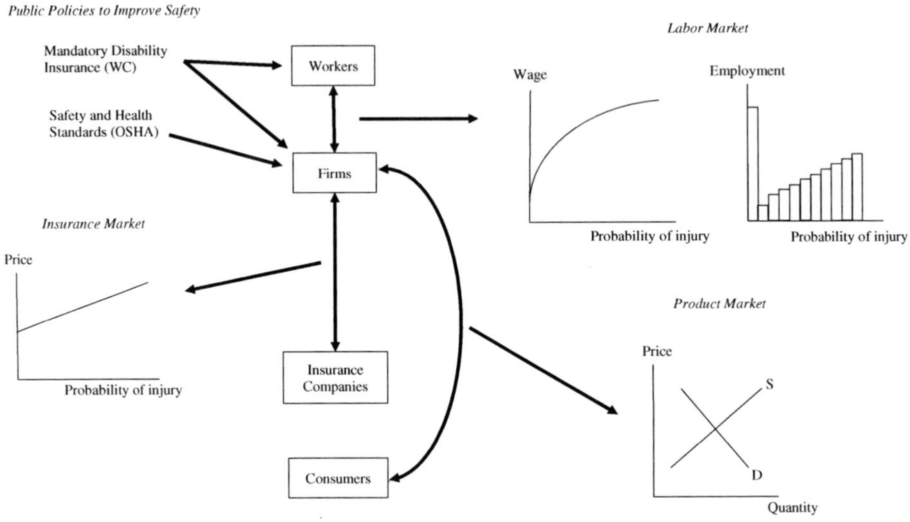

Fig. 5.1 Safety policy interactions.

product, and insurance markets as tempered by government intervention focuses on how changes in safety policy alter labor market outcomes. They realistically allow workers to have differing views about risk and firms to have differing capabilities to produce a safe working environment. Firms unwilling or unable to eliminate all job hazards must pay higher wages to attract workers away from firms offering complete safety. The relationship between wages and risk, the hedonic wage function, adjusts to match workers to jobs so as to equalize the supply of workers with the demand for their services along the entire risk spectrum.

5.1 Parameterizing the Simulation Model

Any method used to solve for the hedonic wage function requires specific functions to represent (i) workers' preferences, (ii) firms' technology, and (iii) interperson and interfirm differences in α and μ (risk aversion and efficiency of safety measures). Figure 5.2 outlines the general approach used to formalize the mathematical model.[1] As

[1] Figure 5.2 is adapted from Figure 5.1 in Shoven and Whalley (1992, p. 104).

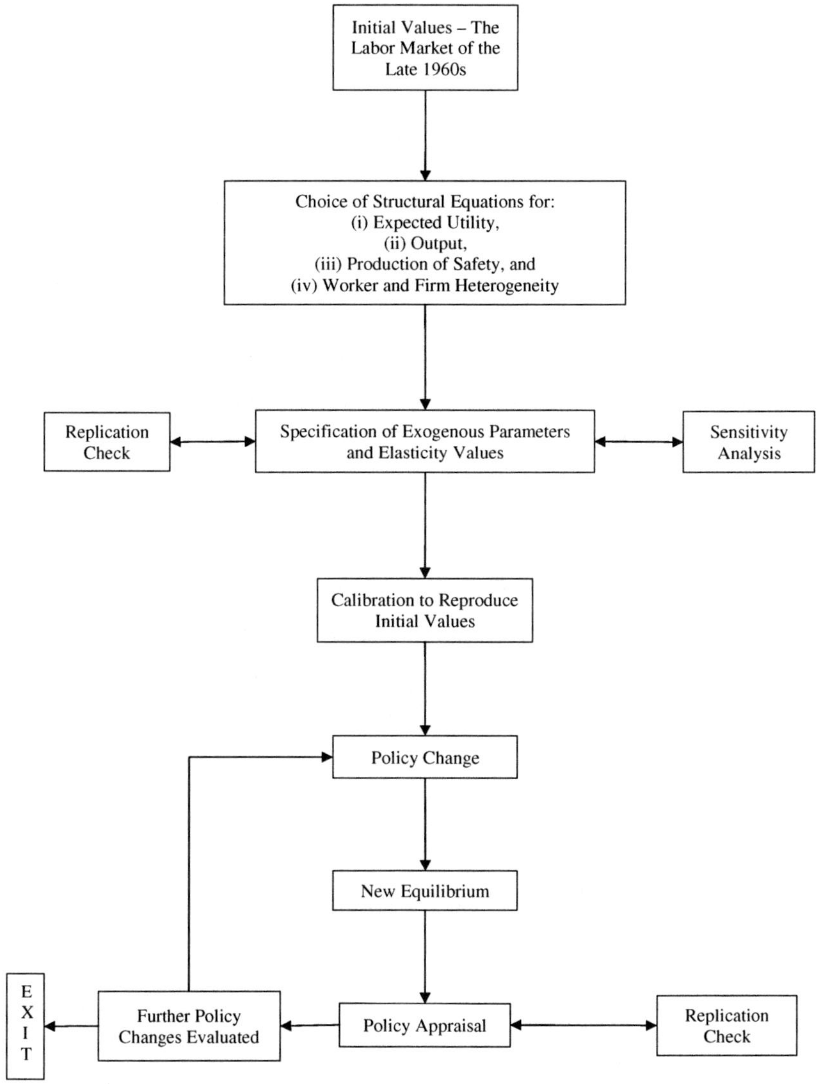

Fig. 5.2 Calibrating the numerical model.

with studies relying on computable general equilibrium they began by specifying a core set of endogenous values the model should reproduce to represent accurately the economy during some base year. They reproduced the labor market at the end of the 1960s, the period just before the major policy initiatives aimed at improving industrial safety, the

Occupational Safety and Health Act and the recommendations of the National Commission on State Workmen's Compensation Laws.

5.2 The Safety Effects of OSHA

Kniesner and Leeth (1989a) examined average OSHA fine of \$763, \$1,528, \$5,492, and \$33,029 (2008 dollars) with the smallest fine representing the actual penalty OSHA imposed on the typical inspected firm in the early 1970s. Their numerical exercise effectively simulates a variety of OSHA activities such as additional inspections, greater violations detected per inspection, and larger fines per violation. Each of the three activities increases a firm's expected fine for violating safety and health standards, which encourages greater safety activities. Because the last three levels of possible OSHA enforcement are quite far from the values appearing in cross-section and time-series data for the United States we would be unwilling to accept econometric forecasts of such extreme changes in OSHA's parameters. (Remember the error associated with an econometric forecast grows with the distance of the independent variables from their sample mean values.) Hence, the numerical simulation results sharpen the empirical picture we have of how OSHA affects labor market outcomes. Additionally, the simulation model allowed Kniesner and Leeth to investigate the important question of why OSHA has failed to improve workplace safety noticeably. Has OSHA been ineffective because of only lax enforcement of safety and health standards or has OSHA been ineffective because of a low economy-wide response rate to safety incentives?

Table 5.1 presents the simulated impact of the four possible levels of OSHA enforcement activities on workplace safety. In each case Kniesner and Leeth (1989a) assumed that WC insurance replaced 50 percent of an injured workers pre-injury wage, a rate equaling the median replacement rate for married men in the early 1970s (Johnson and Wai, 1980). OSHA increases workplace safety but the impact is large only with extreme levels of enforcement. Specifically, imposing an OSHA program with an average fine of \$763 (an expected fine of \$76) reduces the frequency of serious injury in the workplace by a mere 0.3 percent; fines of \$1,528 and \$5,492 reduce the average

Table 5.1. Simulation results: The percent effects of OSHA enforcement activities on the likelihood of work-related injuries.[a]

Average fine for OSHA safety and health violations	Average frequency of injury (%)	Largest probability of injury (%)
\$763	−0.31	−0.19
\$1,528	−0.62	−0.37
\$5,492	−2.28	−1.37
\$30,814	−14.17	−8.66

[a]Percentage changes from the absence of OSHA.
Source: Kniesner and Leeth (1989b), Table 3. Table 1 there lists the functions and parameter values used in the numerical simulations.

frequency of injury by only 0.6 and 2.3 percent. Only the largest average fine produces a significant improvement in workplace safety. Imposing a \$30,814 fine for violating safety and health standards reduces the frequency of injury by just over 14 percent.

As noted, econometric research has discovered at best weak relationships among measures of OSHA activities and industrial injury rates (Ruser and Smith, 1991; Ruser and Butler, forthcoming). Based on the calculations of Kniesner and Leeth (1989a), OSHA's regulatory impotence is not surprising; even vigorously enforced safety and health standards do not dramatically reduce injuries. Apparently, to reduce serious accidents and diseases by 2 percent requires more than a 700 percent increase in fines from the initial OSHA level of \$763. A 14 percent reduction requires more than a 4,000 percent increase in fines. The fundamental problem with OSHA is the extremely low labor market response rate to changes in the economic incentives to expand safety. The low response rate occurs in part because OSHA enforcement activities alter the hedonic wage locus leading to an increase in employment at moderate levels of risk. The employment rebalancing partially counteracts the safety effects at the highest levels of risk seen as the higher fines eliminate some very risky jobs, the highest probability of injury falls.

5.3 The Safety Effects of Workers' Compensation Insurance

WC insurance influences workplace safety in two conflicting ways. Higher benefits for income loss if injured reduce workers' monetary concerns with injury leading them to accept higher risk jobs. In the other direction, higher benefits raise firms' costs of workplace injuries leading them to provide greater safety. The more closely insurance companies match WC premiums to workplace safety the greater are firms' financial incentives to provide safer work environments.

Kniesner and Leeth (1989a) used three higher income replacement rates from the median rate existing in the early 1970s to investigate the labor market effects of WC benefits — 80, 100, and 150 percent. The 80 percent replacement rate reflects the recommendation of the National Commission on State Workmen's Compensation Laws. The two higher rates represent complete protection and substantial overprotection against income loss from a work-related injury. By using two higher rates of income replacement they could investigate much larger changes in WC benefits than possible from econometric estimates with existing data. Moreover, in their research the causality clearly runs *from* WC benefit changes *to* workplace safety changes. By simulating the complete set of labor market adjustments to changes in WC their numerical results provide an important addition to the quantitative picture of how WC insurance benefits affect workplace safety.

Table 5.2 presents the impact of the three higher levels of WC benefits on workplace safety in the absence of any federally imposed safety and health program. In each case there is a positive association between WC benefits and the average frequency of injury. Raising WC benefits to the level suggested by the National Commission on State Workmen's Compensation Laws increases the average injury rate by 0.43 percent. Complete coverage increases injuries by 0.67 percent, whereas overcompensating income loss raises injuries by about 1.2 percent. The results in Table 5.2, which are from a WC system with no experience rating, are consistent with the observed positive association between WC benefits and workplace injury rates across states.[2]

As seen with OSHA, changes in WC also generate two opposing forces. The expansion of benefits attracts more workers to high-risk

[2] The implied elasticity of π with respect to the rate of income replacement seems to be much smaller than suggested by the econometric literature; one possible reason for the difference is miscalculation of injuries as work related in the data used in the econometric research cited.

Table 5.2. Simulation results: The percentage effects of workers' compensation benefits on the likelihood of a work-related injury.[a]

Rate of income replacement under WC	Average frequency of injury (%)	Largest probability of injury (%)
0.8	0.43	0.24
1.0	0.67	0.38
1.5	1.17	0.69

[a]Percentage changes from a 0.5 rate of income replacement under WC.
Source: Kniesner and Leeth (1989a), Table 6. Table 1 there lists the functions and parameter values used in the numerical simulations.

employment in turn increasing the maximum probability of injury observed in the labor market, but the re-equilibrating of the hedonic wage function causes work injuries to fall at moderate risk levels. The resorting of workers moderates to some extent the expansion of injuries in the most hazardous worksites.

Historically, WC insurers have not used the accident experience of a small establishment to determine the establishment's price of WC insurance. Instead, they have combined the injury statistics for all workers within an industrial class and determined a so-called manual rate for WC coverage. The product of each worker's wage rate and the manual rate for his or her industrial class summed over all workers determines the total WC insurance premium for a small firm. As firm size increases insurers pay less attention to the average experience of the industrial class (the manual rate) and more attention to the safety record of the individual firm. Experience rating of insurance policies refers to the process of adjusting insurance prices to reflect individual versus group experience. Insurance providers have completely experience rated WC premiums for only the largest establishments.

Some researchers have suggested that a lack of complete experience rating contributes to the positive relationship observed between injury rates and WC benefits (Ruser and Butler, forthcoming). In their initial simulations Kniesner and Leeth (1989a) assumed insurance prices reflected only group experience. To examine the impact of experience rating Kniesner and Leeth recomputed hedonic equilibrium for the situation in which insurance prices completely reflect the expected frequency of injury within a given establishment. Unlike in the base case of incomplete experience rating, they found when there is complete experience rating of insurance premiums more generous WC benefits *improve* workplace safety. Because experience rating expands the impact of WC benefits on firms' marginal cost of injuries the resorting of firms toward greater safety dominates, in equilibrium, the resorting of workers toward less safe jobs. Increasing WC benefits to the level recommended by the National Commission on State Workmen's Compensation Laws reduces injuries by 8 percent and overcompensating income loss decreases injuries by 26 percent. In comparison, marginally enforced OSHA safety and health standards seem to reduce injuries by 0.3 percent and stringently enforced standards reduce injuries by 14 percent. With complete experience rating of WC insurance premiums, the safety-enhancing effect of WC greatly exceeds that of OSHA in a complete hedonic labor market equilibrium setting.

The simulation results with complete experience rating are in line with empirical estimates in Moore and Viscusi (1990) who find that WC benefits reduce fatal injuries by about a third with the biggest reduction in fatalities occurring at large firms, which are experience rated. Although not presented here, Kniesner and Leeth also find a substantial wage offset from WC benefits as do Moore and Viscusi. Both set of results vary from other research that finds WC benefits generally expanding injuries. Moore and Viscusi argue their examination of fatalities instead of non-fatal injuries allows them to find the true impact of WC on safety. Higher WC benefits not only alter workers and firms incentives with respect to safety, they also alter workers incentives to file for benefits if injured or even if not injured. As shown by Kniesner and Leeth (1989b) the false reporting of injuries to receive more generous WC benefits can easily swamp the true impact on safety, resulting in a positive association between WC benefits and nonfatal workplace injuries.

6

Conclusion

We have examined theoretically and empirically the properties of the equilibrium wage function and its implications for policy. Our emphasis has been of how the researcher approaches research and policy questions when there is labor market heterogeneity leading to a set of wages rather than a single wage that results from an enriched representation of labor market equilibrium. We focus on the application where hedonic models have been most successful at clarifying policy relevant outcomes and policy effects, that of the wage premia for fatal injury risk. The estimates of the overall hedonic locus that we discuss imply the so-called value of a statistical life (VSL) that is useful as the benefit value in a cost-effectiveness calculation of government programs to enhance personal safety. We have demonstrated estimates of the overall hedonic wage locus, which yield a value of statistical life of about $6 million. Among the additional econometric results worth remembering are that there are multiple dimensions of heterogeneity in VSL, including by age and consumption plans, the latent trait that affects wages and job safety setting choice, and family income levels to name a few.

Simulations of hedonic market outcomes are also valuable research tools. As a demonstration of the additional usefulness of giving detail to the underlying structure we not only develop the issue of welfare comparisons theoretically but we also illustrate how numerical simulations of the underlying structure can also be informative. Using a reasonable set of primitives we see that job safety regulations are much more limited in their potential for improving workplace safety efficiently compared to mandatory injury insurance with experience rated premiums. The simulations reveal how regulations incent some workers to take more dangerous jobs, while workers' compensation insurance does not (or less so).

In a future companion piece we tackle the complex econometric issues related to the valuable exercise of attempting to let the data reveal firms and workers' objective functions econometrically and the additional policy issues that such econometric estimates pin down. This is key to understanding why some econometric applications of the hedonic equilibrium model have been less successful in locating the expected wage tradeoff effects of fringe benefits, such as pensions or health insurance.

References

Abowd, J. and D. Card (1989), 'On the covariance structure of earnings and hours changes'. *Econometrica* **57**, 411–445.

Aldy, J. E. and W. K. Viscusi (2008), 'Adjusting the value of a statistical life for age and cohort effects'. *Review of Economics and Statistics* **90**, 573–581.

Arellano, M. and S. Bond (1991), 'Some tests of specification for panel data: Monte Carlo evidence and an application to employment equations'. *Review of Economic Studies* **58**, 277–297.

Ashenfelter, O. (2006), 'Measuring the value of a statistical life: Problems and prospects'. *Economic Journal* **116**, C10–C23.

Ashenfelter, O. and M. Greenstone (2004), 'Estimating the value of a statistical life: The importance of omitted variables and publication bias'. *American Economic Association Papers and Proceedings* **94**, 454–460.

Black, D. A. and T. J. Kniesner (2003), 'On the measurement of job risk in hedonic wage models'. *Journal of Risk and Uncertainty* **27**, 205–220.

Borjas, G. (2010), *Labor Economics,* Fifth Edition. New York, NY: McGraw-Hill/Irwin.

Breyer, S. (1993), *Breaking the Vicious Circle: Toward Effective Risk Regulation.* Cambridge, MA: Harvard University Press.

Brown, J. N. and H. S. Rosen (1982), 'On the estimation of structural hedonic price models'. *Econometrica* **50**, 765–768.

Chetty, R. (2006), 'A new method of estimating risk aversion'. *The American Economic Review* **96**, 1821–1834.

Dorsey, S. and N. Walzer (1983), 'Workers' compensation, job hazards, and wages'. *Industrial and Labor Relations Review* **36**, 642–654.

Eeckhoudt, L. R. and J. K. Hammitt (2001), 'Background risks and the value of a statistical life'. *Journal of Risk and Uncertainty* **23**, 261–279.

Ehrenberg, R. G. and R. S. Smith (2009), *Modern, Labor Economics, Theory and Public Policy,* Tenth Edition. Boston, MA: Pearson Education, Inc.

Ekeland, I., J. J. Heckman, and L. Nesheim (2004), 'Identification and estimation of hedonic models'. *Journal of Political Economy* **112**, S60–S109.

Epple, D. (1987), 'Hedonic prices and implicit markets: Estimating supply and demand functions for differentiated products'. *Journal of Political Economy* **95**, 59–80.

Evans, M. F. and V. K. Smith (2010), 'Measuring how risk tradeoffs adjust with income'. *Journal of Risk and Uncertainty* **40**, 33–55.

Frank, R. H. and C. R. Sunstein (2001), 'Cost-Benefit analysis and relative position'. *University of Chicago Law Review* **68**, 323–374.

Graham, J. D. (2008), 'Saving lives through administrative law and economics'. *University of Pennsylvania Law Review* **157**, 395–540.

Greene, W. H. (2008), *Econometric Analysis.* Upper Saddle River, NJ: Prentice Hall, fifth edition.

Griliches, Z. and J. A. Hausman (1986), 'Errors in variables in panel data'. *Journal of Econometrics* **31**, 93–118.

Hahn, J., J. Hausman, and G. Kuersteiner (2007), 'Long-difference instrumental variables estimation for dynamic panel models with fixed effects'. *Journal of Econometrics* **140**, 574–617.

Harris, J. E. (1979), 'Pricing rules for hospitals'. *The Bell Journal of Economics* **10**, 224–243.

Hwang, H., W. R. Reed, and C. Hubbard (1992), 'Compensating wage differentials and unobserved productivity'. *Journal of Political Economy* **100**, 835–858.

Johansson, P. O. (2002a), 'On the definition and age-dependency of the value of a statistical life'. *Journal of Risk and Uncertainty* **25**, 251–263.

Johansson, P. O. (2002b), 'The value of a statistical life: Theoretical and empirical evidence'. *Applied Health Economics and Health Policy* **1**, 33–41.

Johnson, W. and H. S. Wai (1980), 'Entitlement to disability benefits from more than one public program'. Syracuse University Health Studies Program, Discussion Paper, March.

Kahn, S. and K. Lang (1988), 'Efficient estimation of structural hedonic systems'. *International Economic Review* **29**, 157–166.

Kaplow, L. (2005), 'The value of a statistical life and the coefficient of relative risk aversion'. *Journal of Risk and Uncertainty* **31**, 23–34.

Kniesner, T. J. and J. D. Leeth (1988), 'Simulating hedonic labor market models: Computational issues and policy applications'. *International Economic Review* **29**, 755–789.

Kniesner, T. J. and J. D. Leeth (1989a), 'Can we make OSHA and workers' compensation insurance interact more effectively in promoting workplace safety: A numerical simulation analysis of hedonic labor market equilibrium'. *Research in Labor Economics* **10**, 1–51.

Kniesner, T. J. and J. D. Leeth (1989b), 'Separating the reporting effects from the injury rate effects of workers' compensation insurance: A hedonic simulation'. *Industrial and Labor Relations Review* **42**, 280–293.

Kniesner, T. J. and J. D. Leeth (1995a), 'Numerical simulation as a complement to econometric research on workplace safety'. *Journal of Risk and Uncertainty* **12**, 99–125.

Kniesner, T. J. and J. D. Leeth (1995b), *Simulating Workplace Safety Policy.* Norwell, MA: Kluwer Academic Publishers.

Kniesner, T. J. and W. K. Viscusi (2003), 'Why relative economic position does not matter: A cost-benefit analysis'. *Yale Journal on Regulation* **20**, 1–24.

Kniesner, T. J. and W. K. Viscusi (2005), 'Value of a statistical life: Relative position vs. relative age'. *American Economic Review: Papers and Proceedings of the American Economic Association* **95**, 142–146.

Kniesner, T. J., W. K. Viscusi, C. Woock, and J. P. Ziliak (2010a), 'The value of a statistical life: Evidence from panel data'. Working Paper, Syracuse University, Center for Policy Research, Number 122.

Kniesner, T. J., W. K. Viscusi, and J. P. Ziliak (2006), 'Life-cycle consumption and the age-adjusted value of life'. *Contributions to Economic Analysis and Policy* **5**. http://www.bepress.com/bejeap/contributions/vol5/iss1/art4.

Kniesner, T. J., W. K. Viscusi, and J. P. Ziliak (2010b), 'Policy relevant heterogeneity in the value of statistical life: New evidence from panel data quantile regressions'. *Journal of Risk and Uncertainty* **40**, 15–31.

Kniesner, T. J. and J. P. Ziliak (2002), 'Tax reform and automatic stabilization'. *The American Economic Review* **92**, 590–612.

Koenker, R. (2004), 'Quantile regression for longitudinal data'. *Journal of Multivariate Analysis* **91**, 74–89.

Lamarche, C. (2010), 'Robust penalized quantile regression estimation for panel data'. *Journal of Econometrics* **157**, 396–408.

Leeth, J. D. and J. Ruser (2003), 'Compensating wage differentials for fatal and nonfatal injury risk by gender and race'. *Journal of Risk and Uncertainty* **27**, 257–277.

Leigh, J. P. and R. N. Folsom (1984), 'Estimates of the value of accident avoidance at the job depend on the concavity of the equalizing differences curve'. *Quarterly Review of Economics and Business* **24**, 55–66.

Lillard, L. and Y. Weiss (1979), 'Components of variation in panel earnings data: American scientists'. *Econometrica* **47**, 437–454.

MaCurdy, T. (2007), 'A practitioner's approach to estimating intertemporal relationships using longitudinal data: Lessons from applications in wage dynamics'. In: J. Heckman and E. Leamer (eds.): *Handbook of Econometrics*, vol. 6A. Amsterdam: Elsevier B.V., pp. 4057–4167.

Moffitt, R. A. (2001), 'Policy interventions, low-level equilibria, and social interactions'. In: S. H. Durlauf and H. P. Young (eds.): *Social Dynamics*. Washington, DC: Brookings Institution Press, pp. 45–82.

Moore, M. and W. K. Viscusi (1990), *Compensation Mechanisms for Job Risks*. Princeton, NJ: Princeton University Press.

Olson, C. A. (1981), 'An analysis of wage differentials received by workers on dangerous jobs'. *The Journal of Human Resources* **16**, 167–185.

Rosen, S. (1974), 'Hedonic prices and implicit markets: Product differentiation in pure competition'. *Journal of Political Economy* **82**, 34–55.

Ruser, J. and R. Butler (forthcoming), 'The economics of occupational safety and health'. *Foundations and Trends in Microeconomics* (http://www.nowpublishers.com/mic).

Ruser, J. W. and R. S. Smith (1991), 'Reestimating OSHA's effects — Have the data changed?'. *Journal of Human Resources* **26**, 212–235.

Shepard, D. S. and R. J. Zeckhauser (1984), 'Survival versus consumption'. *Management Science* **30**, 423–439.

Shogren, J. F. and T. Stamland (2002), 'Skill and the value of life'. *Journal of Political Economy* **110**, 1168–1173.

Shoven, J. B. and J. Whalley (1992), *Applying General Equilibrium*. New York: Cambridge University Press.

Sojourner, A. (2010), 'Partial identification of willingness-to-pay using shape restrictions with an application to the value of a statistical life'. Industrial Relations Center, University of Minnesota (Twin Cities Campus), Working Paper 0110.

Solon, G. (1986), 'Bias in longitudinal estimation of wage gaps'. National Bureau of Economic Research, Technical Working Paper 58.

Solon, G. (1989), 'The value of panel data in economic research'. In: D. Kasprzyk, G. Duncan, G. Kolton, and M. P. Singh (eds.): *Panel Surveys*. New York: John Wiley and Sons, pp. 486–496.

Spengler, H. and S. Schaffner (2006), 'Using job changes to evaluate the bias of the value of a statistical life'. Unpublished paper, Darmstadt University of Technology, March.

Sunstein, C. R. (2004), 'Are poor people worth less than rich people? Disaggregating the value of statistical lives'. AEI-Brookings Joint

Center for Regulatory Studies (Washington, DC), Working Paper No. 04-05, January.

U.S. Department of Transportation, Office of the Assistant Secretary for Transportation Policy (2005). Revised Departmental Guidance: Treatment of the Value of Preventing Fatalities and Injuries in Preparing Economic Analyses. Washington, DC.

U.S. Office of Management and Budget (2003). OMB CIRCULAR A-4, Regulatory Analysis (Rep. No. A-4). Washington, DC.

Viscusi, W. K. (1979), *Employment Hazards: An Investigation of Market Performance.* Cambridge: Harvard University Press.

Viscusi, W. K. (1981), 'Occupational safety and health regulation: Its impact and policy alternatives'. In: J. P. Crecine (ed.): *Research in Public Policy Analysis and Management*, vol. 2. Greenwich, CT: JAI Press, pp. 281–299.

Viscusi, W. K. (1993), 'The value of risks to life and health'. *Journal of Economic Literature* **31**, 1912–1946.

Viscusi, W. K. (2003), 'Racial differences in labor market values of a statistical life'. *Journal of Risk and Uncertainty* **27**, 239–256.

Viscusi, W. K. (2004), 'The value of life: estimates with risks by occupation and industry'. *Economic Inquiry* **42**, 29–48.

Viscusi, W. K. (2009), 'The devaluation of life'. *Regulation and Governance* **3**, 103–127.

Viscusi, W. K. and J. Aldy (2003), 'The value of a statistical life: A critical review of market estimates throughout the world'. *Journal of Risk and Uncertainty* **27**, 5–76.

Viscusi, W. K. and W. Evans (1990), 'Utility functions that depend on health status: Estimates and economic implications'. *American Economic Review* **80**, 353–374.

Viscusi, W. K. and J. Hersch (2001), 'Cigarette smokers as job risk takers'. *Review of Economics and Statistics* **83**, 269–280.

Viscusi, W. K. and J. Hersch (2010), 'Immigrant status and the value of statistical life'. *Journal of Human Resources* **45**, 749–771.

Weiss, Y. and L. A. Lillard (1978), 'Experience, vintage, and time effects in the growth of earnings: American scientists, 1960–1970'. *Journal of Political Economy* **86**, 427–447.

Woittiez, I. and A. Kapteyn (1998), 'Social interactions and habit formation in a model of female labour supply'. *Journal of Public Economics* **70**, 185–205.

Wooldridge, J. M. (2002), *Econometric Analysis of Cross-Section and Panel Data.* Cambridge, MA: The MIT Press.

Ziliak, J. P. (1998), 'Does the choice of consumption measure matter? An application to the permanent-income hypothesis'. *Journal of Monetary Economics* **41**, 201–216.

CPSIA information can be obtained at www.ICGtesting.com
Printed in the USA
BVOW012004231212

308908BV00002BA/18/P

9 781601 983701